# PACIFIC
## THE BOUNDLESS OCEAN

Konecky & Konecky
150 Fifth Ave.
New York, NY 10011

This edition published by special arrangement with Vilo Diffusion
Copyright © 1995 Vilo
All rights reserved
ISBN: 1-56852-239-8
Printed and bound in Spain

# PACIFIC
## THE BOUNDLESS OCEAN

TEXTS AND PHOTOGRAPHS
**ALAIN CHENEVIERE**

EDITOR IN CHIEF
**ROGER SABATER**

KONECKY&KONECKY

# INTRODUCTION

Pacific! A magic word conjuring up journeys to far-off lands and exotic discoveries and which has, since the 16th Century, nourished the dreams of generations of sailors and adventurers alike. Impressed by the calmness of its waves, Magellan gave it its name in 1520. Even today this magic name evokes for everyone the vision of paradise here on earth. The popular image, taken up by the cinema in the 20th Century, then by the advertising media, has taken hold of the Pacific and idealized its fine-sand beaches shaded by coconut trees gently swaying in the breeze, its sumptuous, multicolour seabeds, its carefree native inhabitants and the legendary beauty of its Polynesian women. The image is further reinforced in the public psyche by the multiplicity of writers, actors, scientists and scholars or wealthy businessmen who, from Stevenson to Brel, from Melville to Gaugin, Gerbaut, Victor, and Brandos alike..., decided to settle on a deserted Pacific island or atoll.

But the Pacific is more than just a place of dreams. It is also and above all a fresh new world where almost everything still remains to be done. The term New World would have suited it much more than it does America since it was the last part of the globe to be discovered by Europeans. It first attracted captains, missionaries and scientists, only to become almost forgotten in the 19th Century. It was not until the beginning of the 20th Century that the world once more showed an interest in this fabulous liquid continent which, at the outset of the 21st Century, has seemingly infinite possibilities from an economic and strategic point of view. To the images of an Eden protected from the sullies of modern civilization and inhabited by populations whose way of life is natural and simple, other names have, however, been grafted. War for one: Pearl Harbour, Tarawa, Guadalcanal, Midway, Kwajalein... Various events have also provided others such as Bougainville or New Caledonia for their copper and nickel mines or their armed fight for independence. And others such as Bikini, Eniwetok and Mururoa, sites of nuclear tests, or Ouvea, Suva, Palau and Alice Springs where minorities found themselves in confrontation with ruling powers. A less idyllic picture than the first.

The aim of this work is not to present the Pacific from the modern, Western point of view with its moral, economic and political values. This book does not present an analysis or enumeration of advantages and drawbacks which shape its present reality and future aspirations; rather it is one which has opted for the poetry and beauty of places and people. Through its unique landscapes, its treasure-trove of flora and fauna, the legends and ways of life of its ocean populations, it has chosen to rediscover the original, traditional and eternal soul of the real Pacific. The ocean is so vast and powerful, the sky so blue, nature so beautiful, that those who are lucky enough to live there cannot be other than different from the rest of mankind. Beyond the shock of civilisations, they have succeeded in maintaining an exceptional and special bond with their environment. This book is an invitation for you to discover a nature which is endlessly fascinating.

# CONTENTS

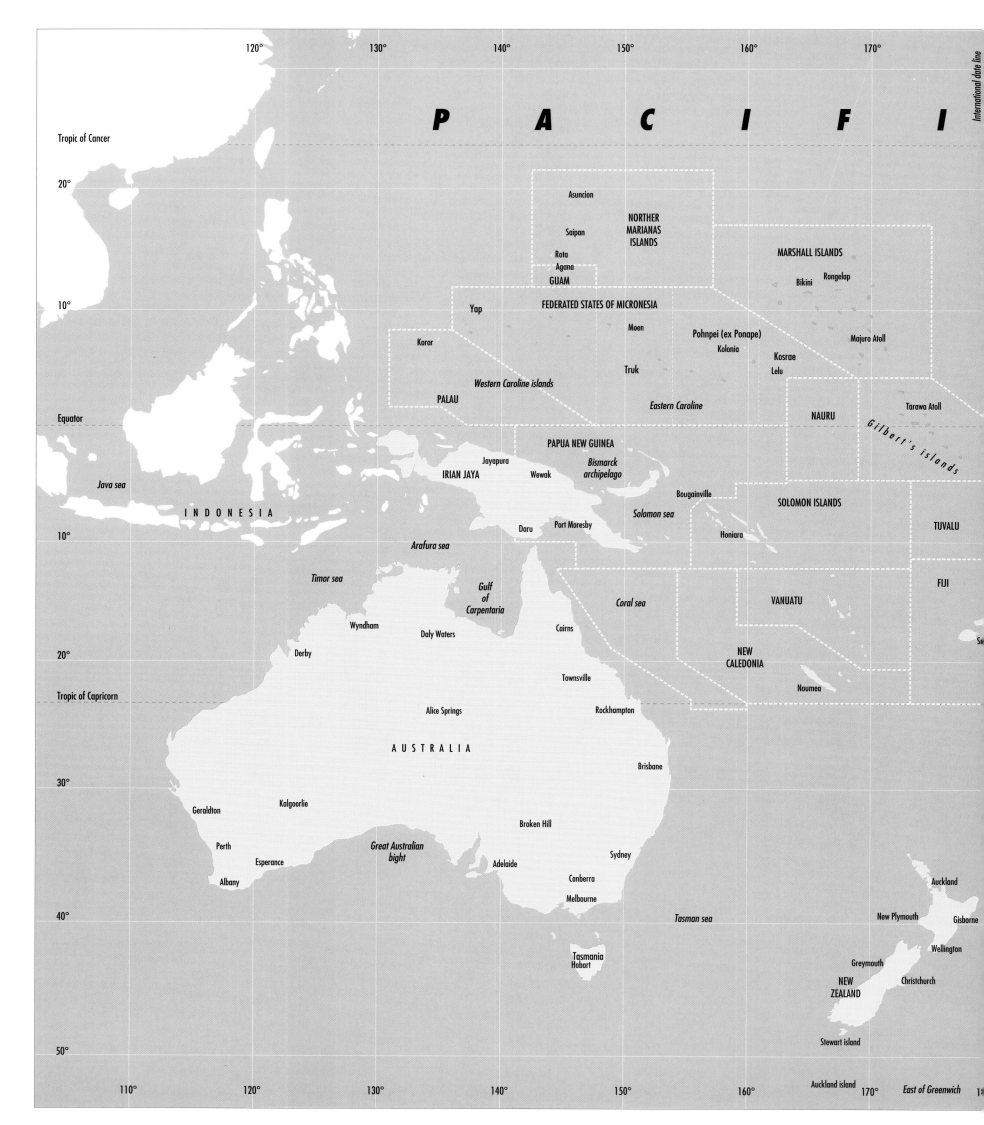

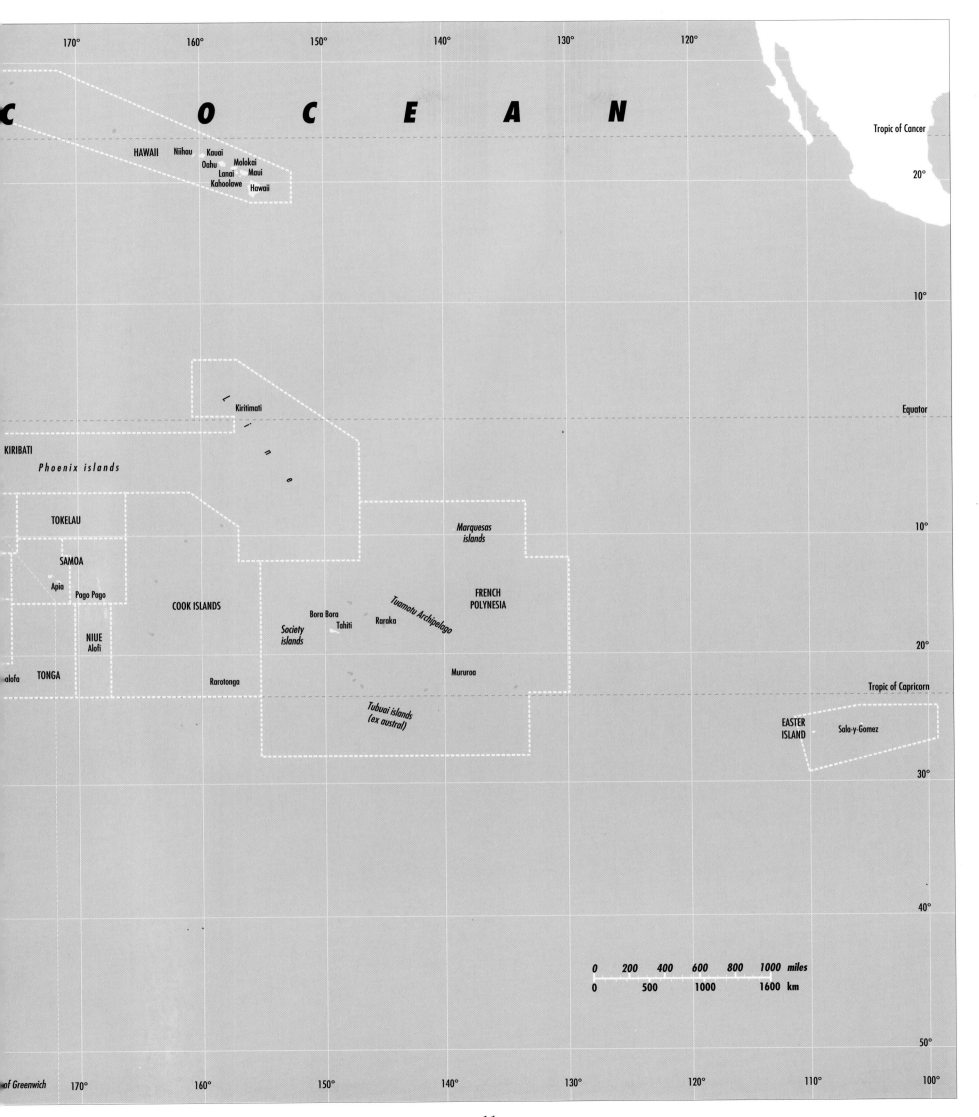

C    O    C    E    A    N

Tropic of Cancer

20°

10°

HAWAII  Niihau  Kauai
Oahu  Molokai
Lanai  Maui
Kahoolawe  Hawaii

Line

Kiritimati

Equator

KIRIBATI

*Phoenix islands*

TOKELAU

Marquesas
*islands*

10°

SAMOA

Apia

Pago Pago

COOK ISLANDS

FRENCH
POLYNESIA

*Tuamotu Archipelago*

Bora Bora
Tahiti

Raraka

NIUE
Alofi

*Society
islands*

20°

alofa  TONGA

Rarotonga

Mururoa

Tropic of Capricorn

*Tubuai islands
(ex austral)*

EASTER
ISLAND

Sala-y-Gomez

30°

40°

| 0 | 200 | 400 | 600 | 800 | 1000 | miles |
| 0 | | 500 | | 1000 | | 1600 | km |

50°

of Greenwich    170°        160°        150°        140°        130°        120°        110°        100°

# 1

# THE PACIFIC OCEAN

The two terms of Pacific and Oceania are often used as synonyms designating a single geographical entity. They do not, however, exactly cover the same reality. The former designates an ocean, the latter describes a geographical compass. In the widest sense of the term, Oceania is considered as the sixth part of the world, the others being Europe, Africa, Asia, America and Antarctica. What is peculiar to Oceania, however, is the fact that, for the majority of it, it is made up of the Pacific ocean, whence the confusion between the two terms.

# DEFINITION OF THE PACIFIC COMPASS

The Pacific ocean is the largest extent of water on earth. Its 180 millions of km² are delimited to the north by Eastern Russia and Alaska, to the east by the American continent, to the south the Austral ocean from which it is separated by the circumpolar current, to the west by China, the insular archipelagoes of South-East Asia and Australia. In its restricted sense, Oceania includes all land masses in the Pacific, a total of just 9 million km², 7.7 million km² of which are made up by Australia alone.

For reasons of simplification, but also because the division reflects geological and human factors, Oceania is divided into five parts; Australia, the major island of New Guinea, numerous archipelagoes and islands contained within three vast entities, Melanesia, Micronesia and Polynesia. Although all the peripheral archipelagoes are situated in the Pacific, like the Aleutians, Japan, the Philippines and Indonesia do not form part of it since they are attached both geologically, historically and ethnologically to the Asiatic continent.

## PACIFIC AND BORDERING SEAS

The underwater morphology of the Pacific is relatively well-known. A contrast is often made between the Pacific itself and the bordering seas. Amongst these, certain are, however, attached to the great Ocean, whereas others are apart. The outer bordering seas to the west (Seas of China, Japan, Celebes, Banda, Philippines) and the north (Seas of Okhotsk, Bering) do not form part of the Pacific. On the other hand, the inner border seas (Seas of Solomon, Coral, Arafura, Tasmania) do. The structure of these latter seas does, nevertheless, show remarkable differences with the Pacific basin itself. Their geography and underwater morphology are much more complex. Their formation is intimately linked to tectonic plate phenomena affecting the Asiatic and Australian continents, whereas the Pacific basin is made up of an oceanic crust which drifts, at an annual rate of approximately 11 cm, in a north-westerly direction, a phenomenon which explains the overall orientation of the archipelagoes. The geological composition of the two zones is also different. Whereas most volcanic effusions in the Pacific basin are of a basaltic type, those of the bordering seas have an andesite aspect, whence the name of the andesite line given to the limit between these two zones which passes right above the major oceanic troughs and trenches bordering on the insular garlands: the trenches of the Aleutians (-25,656 feet), the Kouriles (-34,577 feet), Japan (-34,026 feet), the Mariana trench (-36,188 feet), and those of the Palaos (-26,692 feet), Yap (-28,198 feet), the Tonga (-34,876 feet) and Kermadec Islands (-31,081 feet).

## THE BOUNDLESS OCEAN

When talking of the Pacific, it is impossible not to resort to using the superlative. It alone covers over one third of the surface of the earth and contains over half the waters of the planet whose climate is inextricably influenced by the ocean.

Half the total evaporation of ocean waters is due to the Pacific and 40% of the rain over the whole globe. It is also the oldest ocean on the earth. It is generally believed to correspond to the primordial Ocean which existed prior to the separation of the continents. It has the deepest underwater relief (mean depth 12,792 feet), the most complex and most uneven, as well as the largest volcanoes (immersed or emerged). Its climate is more stable than that of other oceans. Its waters are significantly warmer than those of the Atlantic since it is pratically sealed off at the north and consequently undergoes little influence from the cold Arctic waters. Finally, in contradiction with its name, its anger, expressed in the form of typhoons and hurricanes, is the most formidable and often the cause of considerable damage.

# GEOLOGY

It is thought that at the end of the Primary period, the emerged landmass formed a single, huge continent called Pangaea. This supercontinent was washed by a single ocean which geographers call Panthalassa and which many consider as the distant but direct ancestor of the Pacific. Towards the beginning of the Secondary period, Pangaea split up under the pressure of deep convection currents and divided into two new giant continents, Laurasia and Gondwana, separated by the opening of the Thetys sea. Panthalassa reduced in size and gave birth to the Indian and Pacific oceans.

## MARGINAL OCEANIA AND TRUE OCEANIA

The continent of Godwana included Africa, Madagascar, North America, Arabia, India, Australia and the Antarctic. Oceania is the result of the splitting-up of Godwana itself some 150 million years ago. From the geological point of view, Oceania is divided into two very distinct zones by an andesitic line, marginal Oceania which includes the ancient Australian and New Guinean substratum and the large Melanesian arc of islands, and Oceania itself, including the archipelagoes of Micronesia and Polynesia. Whereas

◀

*Rocky formations*
*on the eastern edges*
*of the Tanami desert heralding*
*the MacDouall Mounts.*

the latter's structure is relatively simple, that of marginal Oceania is very complex, as it is the centre of numerous fracture zones, faults and trenches. It arose from the expansion followed, as the result of the effects of magma currents, by the fragmentation of the immense New Guinean shelf and the geosyncline forming its eastern limit, in the Paleozoic-Mesozoic period. Situated inside marginal Oceania is the Australian shield, the inner and outer Melanesian belts.

The continent of Australia rests on an ancient substratum, New Guinea, the archipelagoes of the Papua group, New Caledonia and New Zealand are part of the inner Melanesian belt and the Bismarck archipelago, the Solomon Islands, Vanuatu and the islands of Fiji and Tonga belong to the outer Melanesian belt.

From a morphological point of view, the Pacific is clearly divided into two very different zones by the andesitic line. To the west of this line, the uneven underwater relief is fragmented into several non-adjacent basins whose emerged sections constitute numerous archipelagoes, lined in a garland shape, and which are in fact the continuation of insular alignments of southern and eastern Asia. The predominance is mainly towards terrigenous deposits. Further to the west, major continental shelves, bearing traces of their temporary emergence during the Quaternary period and overloaded with terrigenous deposits surround Australia, New Zealand and New Guinea. To the east of the andesitic line on the other hand, submarine relief is made up of huge intercommunicating basins whose sediments are of planktonic origin.

## GEOPHYSICS

Apart from Australia which is a continent in its own right, the Pacific is the only liquid continent on the globe strewn with islands of varying shapes and sizes.

### ISLAND TYPOLOGY

The Pacific island formations may be divided into two categories according to physical morphology: continental islands and exclusively volcanic islands to which, more often than not, a coral reef is attached. The former are situated in the western Pacific. They are called continental on account of their isolation following the collapse of older vaster land of a continental type or movement of small plates. They are large mountainous islands of rocky formation, jagged relief and highly eroded, such as New Zealand, New Caledonia, the Solomon Islands and Vanuatu. From the point of

view of their geological structure, the old deposits are interspersed with more recent eruptive rocks. They are often the centre of intense volcanic activity and fall right into the "firebelt" fracture line. The more numerous, exclusively volcanic islands are situated in the centre and in the east of the Pacific, such as the Fiji, Tonga, Samoa, Cook, Society, Marquesas and Hawaiian islands. These are tall, young islands made up of lava strata accumulated over the ages. Volcanic activity is often pronounced, as in the Hawaiian group. Around these islands or on their site when they have become submerged, there are innumerable coral reefs. Oceania numbers over three-quarters

of the atolls in the world. They are to be found everywhere in the Pacific, but are most concentrated in the north-west (Micronesia) and the south-east (Polynesia). These for the most part old coral constructions do, in some cases, border on the coasts of continental islands or volcanic ones that have submerged, or appear at the top of underwater formations which have never emerged. When the original island is still present, a lagoon separates it from the barrier reef in which channels of varying depth are opened.

*Leaden skies herald a tropical storm and roll in over Kahana bay, in Tongatapu and the small islands of Talakite and Mata'abo.*

◄

*Orchids and stems of wild vanilla in the centre of Tahiti. Originally from South America, vanilla was imported into Polynesia in 1848.*

# CLIMATOLOGY

The fact that the Pacific bestrides the equator gives it a relatively stable climate but which is, however, often influenced by the South American niño effect. Between the tropics, air and water temperatures remain around 24°C, with a warmer zone (around 28°C) north of Melanesia. Beyond the high-pressure zones around the tropics, in northerly and southerly directions, temperatures drop very quickly and are influenced by Arctic and Antarctic polar fronts. Rainfall is greater on the northern border of the Equator and especially in the western third of the Pacific between the tropics. This is due to the fact that all of the west zone is subject, in differing degrees, to South-East Asian monsoons which disturb the trade wind system and reinforce local climatic characteristics. The trade winds govern the Pacific's climatic variations. They are, however, themselves affected by the thermal displacement of the Equator throughout the year. During spring and autumn, which are short transitional seasons, they stabilize between the geographical Equator and one of the tropics (Cancer in spring, Capricorn in autumn). At this moment trade winds of the two hemispheres clash in an intertropical convergence zone, giving rise to heavy downfalls of rain, whirlwinds and various atmospheric disturbances. In summer and winter on the other hand, the thermal equator travels quickly between the tropics. During the short periods around the equinoxes, the trade winds become one single equatorial wind coming from the east and bringing with it a more peaceful climate with relatively little rainfall. The Pacific is well-known for the frequency and violent nature of its typhoons. These tropical storms are in fact strong barometric depressions which come about during the northern summer near to the intertropical convergence zone, noteably in western Micronesia and French Polynesia.

The typhoons progress in a north-westerly direction, where they are joined by the monsoons at the beginning of the summer. They then reach the continent which they ravage with winds of up to 360 km/h (215 mph). At the end of the summer, they go north and progressively blow themselves out. The narrow equatorial strip is unaffected by typhoons. The southern hemisphere has relatively few since here the convergence zone is not very far from the geographical Equator. With the exception of Australia, the south of which has a temperate climate, and the centre-west with an arid, desert type climate, as well as New Zealand with its temperate, oceanic climate, all Oceanian islands are situated in the intertropical zone. Consequently they enjoy a warm climate with small temperature ranges. Nevertheless, in mountainous islands, temperatures drop quickly with height. Although close to the Equator, certain summits of New Guinea at almost 15,000 ft have perpetual snow. There is generally little or rare rainfall on atolls and low islands. On mountainous islands on the other hand, rain is frequent and much more abundant. East-facing mountain slopes, on the windward side of the trade winds, receive much more water that their western counterparts.

# FLORA AND FAUNA OF THE EARTH AND AIR

As with the climate, a distinction must be made between Australia and the other Oceanian islands. The variety of species which can be found on the former is in contrast to the relatively poor variety of the latter, which increases the further east one goes. The following passages will deal with the overall lines and characteristics of flora and fauna in the region.

Australia, New Guinea and New Zealand were cut off from the Asian continent from which they are not very far by the Wallace line which radically separates Asiatic placentary mammals from the world of Oceanian marsupials and monotremes, thereby explaining the poor variety of flora and fauna on other islands. In Australia, isolated since the tertiary era, in New Guinea and New Zealand, there is an abundance of vegetable and animal species, many of which are unique or represent veritable living fossils. There is an exceptional mixture of indigenous species and others imported from Asia in particular and sometimes from America. Vegetation is closely influenced by relief. Mountainous islands have a remarkable four-tiered vegetation.

From sea level up to 3,300 ft the wet, equatorial-type forest dominates, with its profusion of high-boled tree varieties (some over 100 feet in height), lianas and other epiphytic plants. Between 3,300 and 9,200 feet are the high tropical forests with their abundant conifers, oaks, beeches and tree ferns. From 9,200 to 12,500 feet the forest thins out to become scraggy and sparse and the moorlands appear. Above these are the the high mountain pastures where there is a mixture of southern, northern and alpine plants.

All these characteristics are much more evident on the eastern windward slopes. It is not uncommon to observe a pluviometric difference which can be as much as three-fold between the two slopes with a shift in the upper limit of each vegetation level

*A common varan lizard, a widespread reptile in Australia.*
*Certain giant species can reach up to 6 feet in length.*

of about 650 feet on average. The original aspect of the Pacific islands has been greatly modified by Oceanian man, then by Europeans, firstly by bringing in plants of foreign origin, from Asia for the most part (yams, taroes, coconut, breadfruit and banana trees), then by altering the natural environment. Species have disappeared, like sandalwood, or others developed anarchically like the guava tree. The same is true for fauna. Apart from the bat, which apparently came by itself, all placentary mammals were introduced by the first Oceanians (dogs, pigs, rats) then by the Europeans (horses, deer, sheep, cattle).

*The Australian crane or "brolga" gets its name from Buralga, a beautiful dancing girl who, according to legend, was changed into a bird by a jealous sorcerer.*

# MARINE LIFE

A study of the aquatic flora and fauna of the
Pacific merits a book in its own right. The aim of
this work is to offer a general overview of the
distribution of different species.

The Pacific makes up the widest extent of water
on earth but, paradoxically, it contains less
vegetable and animal varieties than other oceans.
In the centre in particular, it is even a marine
desert. This phenomenon may be explained by
the fact that there is very little land in the middle
of such an expanse of water and it is known that
in order to live and develop, different species are
encouraged by having a solid support, even if this
be an underwater one. The greater the number of
ecological niches, the more diverse the species. It
must never be forgotten that the underwater flora
and fauna of the Pacific are subjected, as much as,
if not more than, their land and air counterparts,
to two gradients of degeneration which combine:
one from west to east, the other from the Equator
to the south (Antarctic zone) and to the north
(Arctic zone).

## THE WEST-EAST GRADIENT

The further one goes from the Asiatic and
Australian continents in an easterly direction, the
rarer landmasses become and the smaller they get
in opposition to the mass of ocean water. This
explains the abundance of different species in the
western Pacific, a complete impoverishment in the
centre and a slightly lesser one to the east, except
when approaching the continent of South America
where the upwelling phenomena of Peru gives
rise to an exceptional richness. In the Great Barrier
Reef over 350 varieties of builder-corals have been
indexed as against about one hundred in Samoa
and less than 10 (three of which represent 80% of
the total population) in the Marquesas. Similarly
1,500 species of fish have been identified around
Australia, 500 in Tonga and only 52 in Hawaii. This
last example illustrates another determining factor
for Pacific flora and fauna. In order for life to
maintain and reproduce itself, a certain calm is
necessary. It is difficult to thrive next to young
volcanic islands which are still active or have only
recently ceased their active phase.

## THE NORTH-SOUTH GRADIENT

Oceanologists generally distinguish three
horizontal ocean "strips" of differing size; the intertropical strip from the Tropic of Cancer to

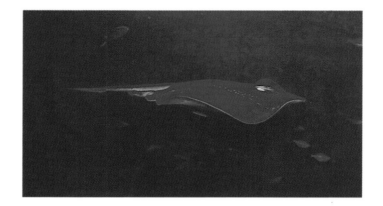

*The warm waters provide
an abundance of large-sized
marine animals,
from mammals
such as dolphins
to fish such as rays
and sharks.*

Capricorn, the temperate strip which includes Tasmania and New Zealand and the sub-Antarctic strip between the south of Tasmania and Stewart island.

## THE INTERTROPICAL ZONE

Warm water and a uniform environment facilitate the development of underwater life, conducive in particular to the thriving Madripores, practically colourless builder-corals. The two dominating groups are the Acropores which construct in branch or table form and the Porites which construct in ball-shape, some of which can reach up to several metres in diameter. There are numerous species of fish which can be divided into two mains groups, bony and cartilaginous fish. The bony varities live in quantities in corals

*A ballet of anthias, small plankton-feeding fishes that live close to reefs, over a coral formation where a few alcyonaria are present, soft corals relatively rare in the Pacific.*

*Fish sometimes have evocative names*
*corresponding to their colours and shapes:*
*a flying scorpion fish, an angel fish in its youthful finery,*
*a pudding-wife and a clown fish separated from its customary sea-anemone.*

or near to reefs: vivid butterfly fish, angel fish with their striped finery and a small spur behind the gills, coral-eating pudding-wife, triggerfish, which can raise the first ray of their back fin, small clown fish that are sheltered by sea-anemones, flying scorpion fish whose spikes contain venom, as well as several fish found at medium-depths like the fearsome barracudas with their powerful jaws and the silver, streamlined scad. There are bony fish that live in the high seas such as bonito and tuna. Cartilaginous fish are represented by rays and sharks. Amongst the twenty or so species of ray, the most well-known are the manta ray which can span up to 12 feet across, the leopard ray whose skin is black with small white speckles, the different whip-tailed sting rays, including the blue-spotted ray and the ray with black markings. There are some 320 species of shark including the famous long-handed varieties, large ocean sharks which come up from the depths and follow shoals of dolphins and tuna, whale-sharks, huge and peaceful beasts sometimes up to 35 feet in length that feed on plankton, and several so-called "reef" species that live near to barrier reefs where they hunt, such as the black- or white-tipped sharks, the grey shark which are fairly inocuous and live in lagoons. Amongst the largest mammals of the intertropical zone are the six species of true whalebone whales including the humpbacked variety which every year, after reproducing in Hawaii, migrate towards the cold waters of Alaska to feed, sperm-whales, grampus and pilot whales and a multitude of dolphins.

## THE TEMPERATE ZONE

This zone is relatively mixed insofar as the only landmasses are in its western part (Tasmania and New Zealand). Elsewhere is the vast ocean which has little life apart from plankton and rare shoals of fish and there is insufficient food to sustain any meaningful sea fauna except of course off Peru where the upwelling phenomenon produces millions of tons of anchovey. Those species that live around Tasmania and New Zealand and south of a line via the Lord Howe islands and Kermadec are not as numerous as in the tropical zone. It is the most southerly limit for builder-corals. Sea-fans abound with their red, orange, yellow and blue colouring to enchant the deeps. There are also many sponges and algae, including the extremely fine green sea lettuce and arborescent eklonias with their strong stipes. Bony fish are represented in particular by the pink or blue mao mao which live in dense shoals in underwater caves and arches, the pig fish with its small pointed mouth,

the thick-lipped moki with its wide black and white stripes. Amongst the cartilaginous fish, apart from several species of shark, including the basking shark which can reach up to 25 feet in length, there are in the temperate waters of the north, two remarkable species: the elephant fish with its large wing-shaped fins and a fearsome predator, the spree, a large scad. Still in the category of large animals and specific to New Zealand are the spermwhale and Hector dolphins.

## THE SUBANTARCTIC ZONE

This zone begins south of a line drawn between the southernmost tip of Tasmania and Stewart island. Its features are just the opposite of the tropical zone. Whereas the latter offers many different species for each of which there are relatively few in number, the subantarctic zone is poor in diversity of vegetable and animal species but rich in quantities. This cold world is dominated by algae. Durvilleas cling to the ocean floor, extending their huge horizontal thongs as well as floating kelp seaweed which can reach 75 feet in height and whose long stipes are maintained in a vertical position by means of small floats filled with carbon dioxide. Near to the Auckland islands, billions of mussels pave the sea floor. There are also millions of squids living in these cold waters which is also home to one of the most dreaded of predators, if ever there was one, the mythical white shark. There are practically no fish in the deeps, except for a few rare species such as the nothotenia, a fish which lives in the deepest waters and has an enormous head. Near to the coasts where they come to rest and reproduce are birds such as penguins and mammals like Hooker sea-lions.

*"Forcipiger"* or long-mouthed,
polyp-plundering butterfly fish.

# ETHNOGRAPHY

Scientific study of Pacific populations is relatively recent and only really began at the beginning of this century, taking off properly after the Second World War. Today, by comparing results obtained from archeology, botany, zoology and linguistics, we can be certain that the Oceanians were of Asiatic origin.

## ARCHEOLOGICAL PROOF

A series of precise archeological researches has been carried out using sophisticated modern techniques such as carbon-14 or thermoluminescent dating, or systematic stratigraphy. The first approach of prehistorians was to work on the oldest certified sites in the vast Asiatic-Sahulian zone. They began in South and East Asia where the first Australoids lived, doubtless originating from central China. Amongst these peoples two human phenotypes had coexisted for a very long period of time. For reasons of simplification, we shall call them "primitive" with negrito features (small in stature, very dark-skinned, fuzzy hair), and "modern" (tall in stature, lighter-skinned, wavy- or straight-haired). Some remarkable excavations, some of which are still underway, prove the antecedence of the South-Asian zone, in particular Malaysia, Indonesia and South China in comparison to the Australo-New Guinean zone with regards to identical tools found dating from the Upper Paleolithic period. It is therefore probable that the first owners of these tools originated from this region of Asia and that some of them migrated east in several successive waves culminating in the two major phases respectively about 45,000 and 18,000 years ago, dates confirmed by archeological discoveries made in Australia and New Guinea. These two periods correspond exactly to the intensest moments of Würms glaciation, which began between 110,000 and 70,000 years ago according to the authors and which ended some 8,000 years ago. During this period of glaciation, the level of water retained by the ice dropped considerably (from 300 to 450 feet depending on the place). Two major continents were then formed, the Sunda which linked most of the southern and eastern archipelagoes (Indonesia, Philippines, Taiwan, Japan) to Asia and the Sahul which included Australia, Tasmania, New Guinea and the bordering continental shelves. The Sunda and the Sahul were separated by a very deep sound where there remained an archipelago from the Primary era, Wallacea, made up of small islands sufficiently near for men, even

*Dani, members of the main ethnic group of Irian Jaya building a drainage network to irrigate fields of yams and taroes.*

with rudimentary means such as rafts, to go easily from one to the other. In the Sahulian zone the two original Australoid human phenotypes have been found once more, with minute differences due to the adaptation to the environment. Thus the ancient man of Kow Swamp in Australia has his Javanese correspondent in Wajak and to the modern man of Australian Mungo (in reality a woman) corresponds the modern man of Solo in Java. The human remains situated throughout the Asiatic zone are all prior to those of the Sahul, which confirms the Asiatic origin of the Australoids. In order to understand the coexistence of the two human phenotypes in question, it has to be admitted that there were already differences way before the first migrations to the east took place some 45,000 years ago.

## LINGUISTIC, BOTANICAL AND ZOOLOGICAL PROOF

The conclusions drawn from archeology are corroborated by other scientific disciplines. Comparative study of languages which almost all belong to the Austronesian family, clearly shows an increasing simplification of syntactic structures of the vocabulary the further east one goes. We know that the older a language, the more complex is its grammatical basis and vocabulary. The population of the Pacific was thus carried out from west to east.

This is also confirmed by botany and zoology. Almost all useful plants brought in by man for his survival, such as the banana, the breadfruit and the coconut trees together with the taro and yam, originated in Asia. The only species to come from the east is the sweet potato which was introduced at a later date in Polynesia, perhaps by Amerindian navigators or more likely via Polynesian traders who reached the American coasts early on. Similarly, all superior mammals, other than those that arrived later with the Europeans living in Polynesia are not indigenous species with the exception of the bat which arrived by itself, but belong to the Asiatic world whence the Oceanian navigators brought them. The pig, the rat and the chicken come from Indonesia and the dog from India.

# THE MAJOR ETHNIC GROUPS

Having established the ethnic origins of the Oceanians, science has tried to define the main ethnological features of the five traditional human groups populating the Pacific, namely the Aborigines, the New Guineans (commonly called Papuans), the Melanesians, the Micronesians and the Polynesians.

## THE ABORIGINES AND THE PAPUANS

These are the descendants of the first populations from a chronological point of view who arrived in the Pacific, perhaps first of all in New Guinea if, as is thought, the first Australoids came from Wallacea from the north-west.

Researchers soon understood that no dissociation should be made between Aborigines of Australia and Papuans of New Guinea, still very close to their remote Australoid ancestors who inhabited the Sahul. The main source of difference resides in the fact that the Aborigines were totally isolated on the Australian continent by the rise in waters following the end of the Würms glaciation approximately 10,000 years ago. Without any contact with the outside world, they have retained two original phenotypes which have given rise to the two types of Aborigines: the Tasmanian, whose last representative died in 1877, and the Australian whose physical differences may be explained by natural evolution linked to the ecology of the living environment and to genetic drifts intrinsic to any human group.

The case of the New Guineans is somewhat different. Unlike their Australian counterparts, they are not considered as a "historical witness". The original phenotypes were significantly changed by migratory waves which, each time, brought new cross-breeding, apart from in the most inaccessible zones. Their skin colour varies from a bluish black to light brown, their stature from the small Pygmy to the tall mountain type.

After multiple quarrels, specialists now agree on two major groups within New Guinea, more or less direct inheritors of the two original phenotypes: the "ancient" negrito type (closely resembling the Sakai of Malaysia and the Philippine Negritoes) where the genetic characteristics of Australian Aborigines are present, in particular in the blood, and the "modern" type, a sort of vast ethnic cluster in which certain groups intermingle with western Melanesians.

## THE MELANESIANS

Prehistorians have determined two major periods in the occupation of the Sahul: the old period from 20,000 to 10,000 BC, characterized by a tradition of rough-core tools, and the recent period from 10,000 to 8,000 BC, marked by a tradition of modern tools where the chips had been removed from finely worked blades. The former characterizes Australoid populations, the second other later populations, for the sake of simplicity called Austronesians, even though there is no Austronesian ethnic reality as such. Austronesian is a linguistic grouping, the most extensive and varied in the world. It stretches from Madagascar to Easter Island. Oceanian languages are part of the whole of Austronesia, within which linguists distinguish a western Austronesian, including Indonesia, the Philippines, Formosa, the western part of Micronesia, and an eastern Austronesian including in particular Melanesia, central and eastern Micronesia and Polynesia. For want of a better term grouping together the different Oceanian populations speaking these languages, ethnologists have gone beyond the strict linguistic framework and admit of an ethnolinguistic Austronesian group whose origins are in South-East Asia.

There Australoids of the negrito type are thought to have mixed with mongoloid invaders from central China, giving rise to Austronesians. Numerous researchers see in the Polynesians distant descendants of this primary cross-breeding in Asia. Some of these pre-Polynesians are thought to have left for the east at the same time as the Melanesians, sometimes even before them. In our present state of knowledge, it would seem that the Melanesians are the result of a second cross-breeding some four millenia later, but in eastern New Guinea this time, between Austronesians and Australoid populations already present. Some four thousand years ago, some Melanesians left the New Guinea coasts to colonize, by stages and in small successive groups, the archipelagoes situated to the east. By the end of the first millenium AD, the last of them reached Fiji, the furthermost lands from the point of departure. As on other islands, they drove out the first inhabitants who were Polynesians.

## THE MICRONESIANS

Often confused with Polynesians, the Micronesians form an original ethnic entity, at least in western Micronesia. For a long time they were considered as the mixture of Polynesian and Melanesian populations via an Asiatic strain (Indonesians, Japanese, Taiwanese). In fact they constitute the least uniform human group in Oceania, whence researchers' uncertainties and hesitations. It is, however, possible to establish a Micronesian type whose origins go back to light-skinned populations (certain specialists affirm that there may have been numerous white-skinned groups within a xanthoderm majority) which left the coasts of China, Vietnam and Taiwan from the fourth millenium BC heading for the small eastern archipelagoes. The oldest certified sites of human remains are in the Mariana islands (Saipan) and Palau. They date from the 16th Century BC but present-day stratigraphic excavations, in particular in Yap, lead us to hope that even older sites will be uncovered. The Micronesian zone is divided into two halves, western and eastern. It is in the west that the most authentic Micronesian type may be recognized with fine, mongoloid facial features, straight hair, of medium stature and light-skinned. To the east, cross-breeding with the Polynesians (strong bone structure, massive build, fuller-featured) disguise numerous original characteristics. Local speech patterns offer a close comparison with ancient Samoan, thereby confirming Polynesian influence.

## THE POLYNESIANS

Our knowledge of the Polynesians is largely due to the discovery in the 60's, followed by the study of the lapita civilization, of the first site where this cultural complex was brought to light in a vast geographical zone stretching from the Bismarck archipelago to Samoa and Tonga, taking in the Solomon Islands, Vanuatu, the Fiji Islands and New Caledonia. Intermingled with Melanesian finds, ancient sites have been unearthed, two of whose distinctive features are a composite pottery decorated with geometric motifs and adzes made out of obsidian of a type unknown in non-lapita sites. Once analysed, these new vestiges proved that they were made by proto-Polynesian populations who, in 1,500 BC, occupied most of the western archipelagoes at the same time as the Melanesians, sometimes even before them. Further studies showed that the "lapitans", doubtless the remote inheritors of the first cross-breeding between Australoids and Austronesians in Asia, were the direct ancestors of present-day Polynesians. These pre-Polynesians were driven out from the western Pacific during the second millenium BC by the dominant Melanesians. Towards 1,500 BC their dugout canoes reached Fiji, at that time uninhabited, then, 200 years later the Samoa and Tonga islands. They stayed there for some one thousand years to become the Polynesians we know today. In the second century BC the arrival of the Melanesians in Fiji and the limited amount of arable land in Tonga and Samoa brought about the great Polynesian diaspora. Some groups migrated to eastern Micronesia (Line, Phoenix, Gilbert and Nauru islands) where they intermingled with the local populations. Most of the others left for the east and settled in central Polynesia (Tokelau, Cook, Marquesas and Society islands) between 200 BC to 300 AD. From here they colonized the rest of the Polynesian triangle along three axes. To the north-east, they reached Hawaii between 300 and 400. To the east they arrived in the Gambier islands around 600 and Easter island one century later. Between 800 and 900, in a south-west direction, others, the ancestors of the present-day Maori, landed in New Zealand.

*Of all the peoples in the Polynesian area, the inhabitants of the Marquesas Islands have best preserved their traditional art. This carver is working on a ritual tiki.*

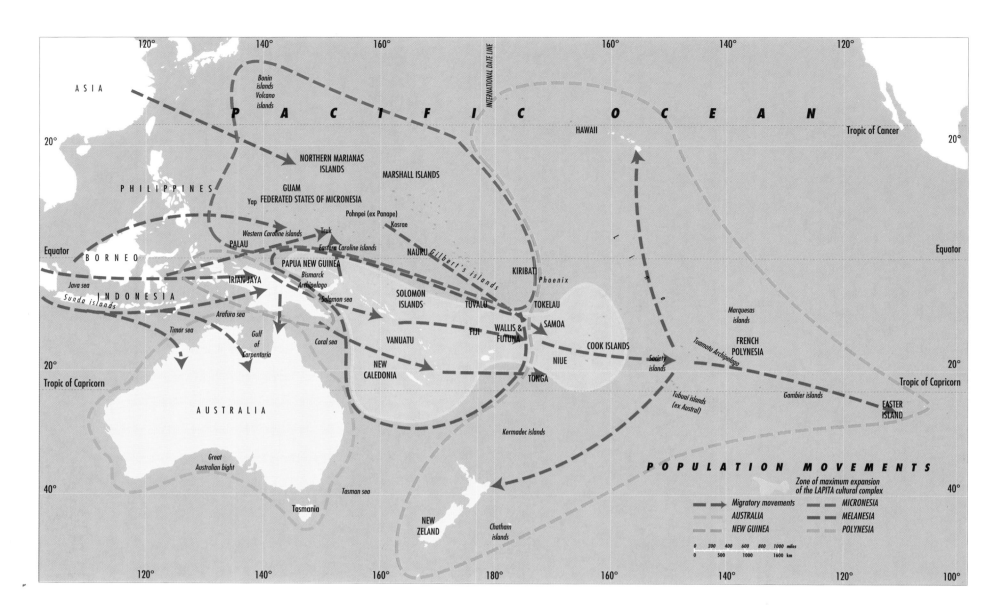

POPULATION MOVEMENTS

Zone of maximum expansion of the LAPITA cultural complex

- - - Migratory movements
- - - AUSTRALIA
- - - NEW GUINEA
- - - MICRONESIA
- - - MELANESIA
- - - POLYNESIA

0    200   400   600   800   1000 miles
0      500      1000      1600 km

*Northern
Aborigine.*

*Western
Aborigine.*

*Papuan
from Irian Jaya.*

*Papuan from central
Papuan New Guinea.*

*Melanesian women from
the Solomon islands*

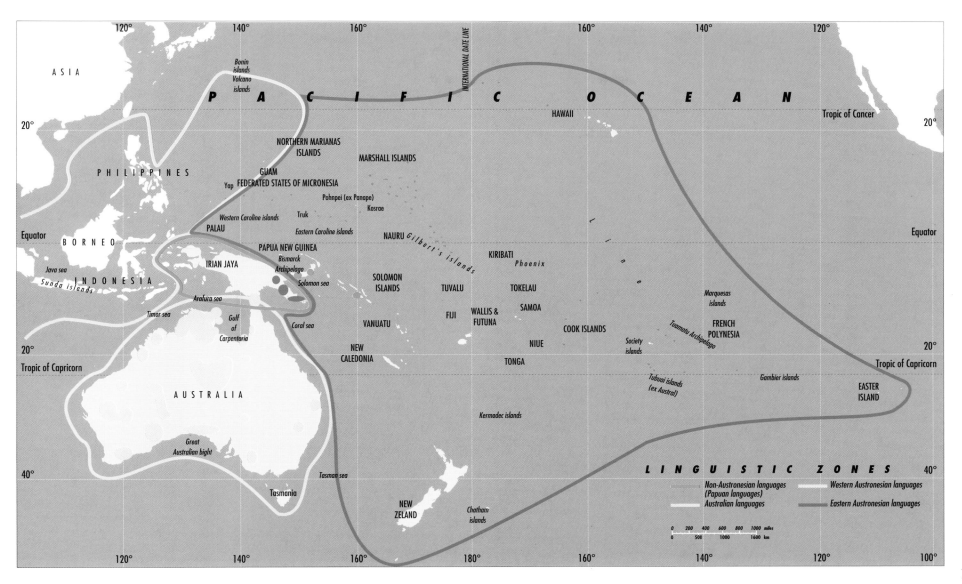

Melanesian from
northern Vanuatu.

A western Micronesian
woman (Truck).

An eastern Micronesian
(Mariana islands).

Polynesian
from the Society islands.

A Polynesian woman
from the
Marquesas islands.

Australia

INDONESIA  120°  130°  140°  150°

Timor sea  Arafura sea  PAPUA NEW GUINEA

10°  •Darwin  Arnhem's land  Gulf of Carpentaria  Torres strait

Cape York Péninsula

Indian ocean  Wyndham  Cooktown  Coral sea

Kimberley  Tanami desert  Cairns

•Derby  Northern territory  Barkly plateau  Gregory ranges

Dampier's land  Townsville

20°  Great Sandy desert  Selwyn ranges

Hamersley ranges  Lake Disappointment  Macdonnell ranges  Queensland  Tropic of Capricorn

Gibson desert  •Alice Springs  Rockhampton

Western Australia  Amadeus Lake  Musgrave ranges  Simpson desert

Robinson ranges  Great Victoria desert  Lake Eyre depression  Charleville  Darling Depression

Sturt desert  Brisbane

Southern Australia  Flinders ranges

30°  Nullarbor plain  •Bourke  Liverpool ranges

Geraldton  Gawler ranges  Port Augusta  New South Wales

•Coolgardie  Great Australian Bight  Adelaide  •Newcastle

Perth  •Sydney

Victoria  Australian Alps  Canberra

Albany  •Melbourne

40°  Australia

Indian Ocean  Tasmania

•Hobart

0  Miles  500

# 2
## 1

# AUSTRALIA

The Commonwealth of Australia, whose administrative capital is Canberra, is made up by the vast Australian continent (7,682,300 km²) and by island territories in the Pacific; the Lord Howe, Norfolk and McQuarie islands, numerous reefs and the Coral Sea Islands Territory, representing one hundred or so km². Although outside our present scope, mention should also be made of islands such as Cocos and Christmas islands in the Indian ocean which come under Australian administration.

## A MASSIVE AND UNIFORM GEOLOGICAL STRUCTURE

The Australian continent is part of a vast expanse of landmass dating back to the Primary era, delimited by two geosynclinal troughs that extended in an immense arc of a circle, called the "westralian" to the west and which reached Timor and the Spice Islands, and the vast "Papua" to the north and east which stretched from present-day New Guinea to New Zealand, taking New Caledonia in on its way. Present-day scientific knowledge leads us to think that it was made up of two major landmasses, Australia to the west and "Tasmantis" to the east which subsequently sank and which were separated by the Tasman trough. Today the Australian continent is itself clearly divided into two structural entities, the old shield covering the whole of the northern half and the Tasman trough to the south as far as Tasmania. The former is a fragment of ancient Gondwana. It was made up from small nuclei which were united during the several major orogenic phases over 1,000,000,000 years ago. Made up essentially from metamorphic rocks (gneiss, cristalline schist) from the Precambrian period, it outcrops almost one third of the Australian territory. Subjected to subsequent orogenic thrusts, in particular from the end of the Silurian period to the Permian, it fractured into several blocks that gave rise to the plateaux, whereas the waters gradually flooded those parts which had slipped, initiating a highly active process of sedimentation that lasted until the onset of the Quaternary period. The thickness of sedimentary layers is generally 9,800 to 11,500 feet but can in some parts reach 23,000 feet, as in the Canning basin.

The Tasman trough appeared during the mid-Cambrian era when the waters withdrew from the Adelaide geosynclinal and flooded eastern Australia. Later the uplift and the folding of the Tasman trough, which took place over a long period from the Carboniferous to the Permian created the Main Barrier range. During the Cretaceous a vast inland sea developed in the centre of Australia, dividing it into two large western and eastern "islands " before drying up. After undergoing strong erosion, the Tasman trough went through a new phase of uplift during the Tertiary, followed by intense volcanic activity during the Quaternary as testified by abundant eruptive formations (granites, syenites, diorites, porphyrites, basalts, trachytes), whereas the centre of the continent was occupied by a vast lake, of which Lake Eyre is the visible remains.

## A VARIED RELIEF

We commonly think of Australia as a uniformly flat continent. In reality it has a wide variety of reliefs. Three major geomorphological expanses may be noted: the plains and high plateaux of the west and centre-west, the centre-east depression and the eastern mountain ranges.

Strewn with the highly eroded vestiges of old mountain formations, the former cover the majority of the land surface. They make up an immense desert plain astride the Tropic of Capricorn. Altitude varies from 650 to almost 2,000 feet. Around the edges are scattered several depressions, such as the Canning Basin to the north-west and the Nullarbor Plain to the south which ends in uninterrupted 300-feet high and 1,500 km-long cliffs overlooking the ocean.

The centre-east is occupied by lowlands, some of which are below sea level, such as the Lake Eyre depression at -35 feet. Two medium mountain areas, the Selwyn Range to the north, the Grey Range and the Main Barrier Range to the south, impart rhythm to the relief by delimiting and separating the central lowlands and the Great Artesian Basin, from the coastal plain of the Gulf of Carpentaria in the north and the alluvial plains of the Murray-Darling in the south-east.

Although there are a few mountain expanses in western Australia (Hamersley and Barley Ranges) and in the centre (MacDonnell and Musgrave Ranges), it is in the east that the major mountain areas are to be found, the major feature being the Great Dividing Range which borders the eastern seabord for 3,500 km from Cape York to Tasmania. Mean altitude is over 3,300 feet and the highest point is Mount Kosciusko, 7,328 feet.

*The dry and dusty plains to the north of Arnhem Land are traversed by the meanders of several rivers, here the eastern Alligator.*

## A CONTINENTAL CLIMATE

The Australian continent is situated in an intertropical zone. The vastness of the territory combined with the Great Dividing Range to the east which halts the ocean influence give rise to a continental climate for most of the country. General atmospheric circulation means that, throughout the year, a mass of tropical air made up of anticyclones which go slowly from west to east, covers the majority of the territory. Australia therefore has a dry climate, arid in the central parts, with only its seaboard areas to the north, south and east receiving rain, particularly in the southern winter. The extreme south as well as Tasmania are subject to maritime influences due to the masses of polar air coming up from the south.

Australia has four major climatic zones: desert, tropical, oceanic and Mediterranean climates. All central parts representing over half the continent have a desert climate. Rainfall is rare and variations in temperature between a very cold winter (July to September) and a very hot summer (January to March) are significant. The tropical climate is to be found in the north and east of the country, including a dry season (around July) and a wet season (around January). Temperatures remain generally quite high throughout the year and rainfall is relatively heavy (1,500 mm of water per year in Darwin, 2,200 mm in Cairns).

The extreme south-east of Australia and Tasmania have an oceanic climate which is cooler, and rain throughout the year. Finally in the central southern and western areas there is a Mediterranean climate with moderate rainfall and temperatures in summer, slight rain and warm temperatures in winter.

◀

*The northern territories
are the "billabong" region.
Considered as sacred
by the Aborigines,
these marshlands with their brackish
water harbour abundant fauna,
particularly rich in bird life.*

## A UNIQUE FLORA AND FAUNA

Australia is one of the most prized countries in the world for botanists and zoologists. The fact that it has been isolated since the Tertiary period has enabled it to preserve vegetable species that appeared in the Primary and certain of which are unique and unknown or have disappeared long ago on other continents, or which simply present an exceptional morphology. There are over 500 species of eucalyptus trees (sometimes reaching 130 feet in height) and no less than 700 species of

*The whole of the northern
coastline and the periphery of
small islands is marked
by mangrove forests
which abound in Rhizophora
mangrove trees.*

acacias. Certain phyla are over-represented, such as angiospermae with 1,200 species, ferns with 260 species, mosses with 600 species and thousands of varieties of mushrooms. Also present is a flora of Malayan origin which can be found noteably in Queensland, the natural front door for Asiatic species (bamboos, orchids), and perhaps one other primitive type, Antarctic in origin. The fact that the majority of the country is subject to drought conditions has produced an essentially xerophilous vegetation, despite the fact that only 5% of the land surface is covered by forests. There are five, unequally divided zones going from north to south. Firstly the humid, tropical forest which has strong equatorial characteristics on the coastal side (mangroves, evergreen plants, ferns, lianas, bamboos). Then the vast bush, covering over half of Australia. This is savanna-type landscape becoming, in parts, stunted and sparse forest with, in addition to a large number of acacias, very uncommon species such as casuarina, bottle tree and kangaroo grass.

The third zone is that of the scrubland, with its numerous dwarf eucalyptus trees and scraggy thorn-bushes. The real desert is to be found in the centre-west only, with the occasional and thin thorn-grass. Finally to the south opens out the major forest zone, tropical in character before changing to a southerly, rain-type one with an abundance of palm trees, arborescent ferns, giant eucalyptuses and conifers.

The isolation of the continent has also been a determining factor in Australian fauna. Some 160 species of mammals have been indexed, unknown or extinct in other parts of the world. The most well-known are the marsupials, with the opossums, koalas and over 50 varieties of kangaroos. Others appear as veritable living fossils, such as monotremes (the spiny porcupine and the duck-billed platypus), lizards such as the moloch and the bearded lizard. Certain birds, such as the emu and the jabiru, are specific to Australia. It is impossible to draw up an exhaustive table of Australian fauna. The figures speak for themselves. Over 100 placentary mammals have been indexed (bats, various rodents, dingoes), 500 birds (where "ancient" species cohabit with modern pelicans, cockatoos, parrots and other lyre birds), 400 reptiles, 110 tailless batracians and over 50,000 insects. The reptiles include flying lizards, skinks, agamas, varanian lizards, crocodiles as well as numerous snakes with deadly venom (the taipan, coral snake, tiger snake, copperhead snake and death adder).

And, of course, that not-to-be-forgotten marvel, the madrapore corals of the Great Barrier Reef, in and out of which swim a myriad of multicoloured fish and sharks, providing shelter for innumerable mollusks, some of which are true prehistoric hangovers. As against the 700 species of mollusks (mussels, large land snails), only 180 varieties of freshwater fish have been indexed. Entire families are missing for a reason which has so far remained unknown. The inland rivers harbour, however, surprising archaic specimens, like the lungfish and the barramunda (dipneusti).

*The emu is a large runner-bird indigenous to the Australian continent.*

*Amongst the numerous varieties of kangaroos, the "large reds" can reach up to 7 feet tall and are dangerous to man when disturbed.*

# THE ABORIGINES

The Aborigine population of Australia is today only 180,000 of which only 70,000 are considered as full blood. Descendants of the first inhabitants of the continent, they represent hardly 1.1% of the total population. Out of the 17,600,000 Australian citizens, 95% come from differing European stock, including 90% of British origin, followed by Italians, Greeks and ex-Jugoslavs with a few contingents of Germans, Dutch and Poles. A small Asiatic minority (Indonesians and Chinese) and Oceanians make up approximately 4% of the population. This situation may be explained in part by the famous 1902 Immigration Restriction Act which made it very difficult for poor Europeans and above all African and Asian populations to enter the country.

## THE ETHNOCIDE OF EUROPEAN COLONIZATION

After being located by the Spaniard Luis de Torres, the Australian continent was discovered in the 17th Century by the Dutch, in particular Jansz in 1606 and Tasman in 1642 who called it New Holland, a name which it retained until towards 1850 when it became known as Australia. The colonization of this vast territory did not, however, begin until the 19th Century when the British suddenly became interested in these far-off lands for economic and strategic reasons. Their stranglehold on Australia gave rise to an ethnocide the like of which few countries have known. When the Europeans arrived, there were an estimated 350,000 Aborigines and a process of systematic annihilation took place which left the road open for settlers and adventurers of all sorts. The British Crown transformed the country into a vast area of penal servitude, dispatching the dregs of its prisons into ever-multiplying penitentiaries. At the same time emerged the establishments and stations where livestock breeding was carried out on a large scale. From 1851, the discovery of gold-bearing deposits provoked a gold rush. For the sole year of 1852, over 100,000 people, a staggering figure for the times, emigrated to Australia. The population doubled in ten years from a little under 500,000 inhabitants in 1851 to over one million in 1861. But, unlike their Maori or Melanesian neighbours, the Aborigines were not warriors. Still living in prehistory with their heads full of mythological dreams, they were helpless to withstand the onslaught of the Whites. They were never able to fight against them, except in sporadic attacks and small uprisings which were quickly crushed. In Tasmania, they disappeared altogether at the end of the 19th Century. On the mainland, there remained only 67,000 in 1933 and only just over 50,000 in 1945. Since the 1967 referendum, they have full citizenship under the Constitution. Their right to a cultural difference is written into governmental programmes and serves mainly to appease the conscience of the white majority. The lands which are given back are practically all situated in desert territory and, for every Aborigine who becomes integrated and succeeds in white society, how many squat in shantytowns on the outskirts of towns? The relatively high birth-rate of Aborigine women is balanced by a strong child mortality rate, despite progress made in hygiene and medical assistance. Average life expectancy for Aborigines is 52 years as against 75 for whites. There was a significant increase in their population between 1945 and 1975, but which seems to have levelled off today. Many analysts feel that the traditional Aborigine people will not survive into a sophisticated 21st Century.

*An Aborigine hunter in resting position.*
*Totally motionless, he can wait thus,*
*inhaling the air to "smell out" game.*

*T*he sky, the earth and the Ocean have always existed. At the beginning of the time of dreams, they had the same shape as they do today. The world was shared between gods and spirits. In the heavens reigned Yhi, the Sun-goddess, Balhoo, the Moon-god, always accompanied by Wahn, his faithful crow and the seven Meamei (Pleiades). The earth was the domain of Tya. On its surface there lived the nurrumbunguttia, male and female spirits who had a vaguely human form. Their life was not an easy one. During the day, the sun burnt them and, at night, they shook with cold. They had no fire and ate their food raw. And so they invented fire to heat themselves and to cook their food. But these glowing lights displeased the gods who sent an immense wave to extinguish them. Unrelentingly, the flood covered the surface of the earth. Many nurrumbunguttia perished by drowning. The others were saved by a wind which carried them to the sky. They hugged those precious embers which they had been able to salvage close to them. When they reached the heavens, the nurrumbunguttia became eternal and were changed into stars. Since they were no longer either hungry, thirsty, hot or cold, they had no more need of their embers. They threw them into the sky where they formed the Milky Way. But some spirits remained angry and resented the gods who had exterminated their race. They refused to be transformed into stars and preferred to wander in the vast sky. They were the causes of storms and cataclysms. The other nurrumbunguttia chose the oldest amongst their number to become gods and take part in the government of the world with the original great gods. The two most important were called Baiame and Pund'jil. They settled in the Milky Way. So the Great Spirit, the celestial hero to whom all gave the name "Father of everything" since he incarnated the virtual principles of all life, was wise and calm, so Pund'jil was quick-tempered and hot-headed. On earth, however, the devastating flood had ceased. The mountains reappeared, then the plains. The ocean found its original place once more. Yhi began again to populate the world with living creatures. In the sky she placed those who flew, in the Ocean those who swam and on earth those who ran, jumped and crawled. She had made them according to the same model, drawing inspiration from the appearance of the ancient nurrumbunguttia. They all therefore had a vaguely human form. And this gave rise to an unimaginable disorder. Although the living creatures had different ways of living and thinking, they looked so alike that they could no longer tell each other apart. In addition, the body which they had been given was poorly adapted to the conditions of the forest, the Ocean or the air. They came to express their grievances to Yhi who accepted to give to each the body that it desired. Thus it was that she gave wings to bat and bird, fins and scales to fish, paws to mammals, rings to snakes and a shell to insects. When she had finished, she noticed two beings who were motionless. They seemed to be afraid and asked for nothing. As they did not answer her questions, the goddess, perplexed, consulted the other gods. It was decided that the two would be made after the image of Baiame and that a soul would be breathed into them made up from a part of the celestial hero. The children of Pund'jil were instructed to carry out the divine mission. Kararok, the son, and Babiger, the daughter, entered their bodies, thereby creating the first man and the first woman. In order to distinguish them from other creatures, Nepelle, master of the heavens, allowed the star Wang to give them a part of the celestial fire. Thus the new humans could warm themselves during the night and cook their food.

As the world was near to its creation, the living creatures that populated it still knew many things that have since been forgotten. For example, men and animals, who had a common origin, spoke the same language. Man understood the snake and spoke to the kangaroo, who could converse with the bird or the fish. Baiame assisted men, his spiritual children, in their knowledge of nature. He chose certain of them to be intermediaries between himself and humanity. It was the wirinun (shamans) who, during their sleep, rose to the sky where they received their divine orders and acquired magical powers. When they came back down to earth, these wirinun guided their brothers along the "paths of dreams". Thus they took them across the whole surface of the earth. Each time they found a source, they planted a stick in the ground and set up a camp which they entrusted to a group of men and women. Under the guidance of their shamans, men

# The legend of Baiame

*The Australian Aborigines draw their numerous myths of the creation from the mystical "Time of Dreams", such as this legend which is famous in the centre and east of the country.*

discovered and colonized the whole earth. They invented civilization.

But the situation grew worse because human beings gradually lost contact with the animals. They killed them, even when they were not hungry, forgetting that they once had a common origin. Weary of these repeated murders, the animals came and complained to Yhi and Baiame. The gods were not inclined to punish men who were their favourite creatures. So the animals went to fiery Pund'jil. They pointed out that if man existed, it was the god who, via his children, was responsible for him. Pund'jil listened and promised to act. He summoned those of the ancient nurrumbunguttia who had remained rebellious and who were wandering in the sky. He ordered them to massacre the men.

The spirits were only too pleased to obey and exact revenge on those who had taken their place on earth. Typhoons, tornados, sandstorms, earthquakes rained down upon wretched mankind who took shelter in caves and under rocks. Many perished. Then Pund'jil in person came down on earth. He cut the survivors into pieces and cast them to the four corners of the universe. Only a few just men were spared thanks to the intervention of Baiame. The gods assembled them together with the representatives of the animals.

Men had to promise not to kill animals except for food. The animals accepted that certain of them should supply the meat which men needed. But the gods, who knew that the promises of yesterday are often forgotten the following day, decided to place all creatures under the law of death. Thus no species, be it vegetable, animal or human, would have sufficient time to destroy the others. This was the price to pay for peace on earth.

*The eastern approaches of Mount Todd.*

From a geographical point of view, Northern Australia stretches from the Kimberley plateau to the Cape York peninsula.

Apart from several islands bordering on the north coast, in particular Bathurst, Melville, Elcho, Wessel, Barrow and Wellesley, it includes the northern third of three states, Western Australia, Northern Territory and Queensland. Considered as the oldest inhabited and most traditional area of Australia, it is the site of numerous Aboriginal settlements within several large tribal confederations, inluding the Djuwali, the Brinken, the Gunavidji, the Wulamba-Murngin, the Tiwi, the Wadaman, the Wogiman and the Jaraldi.

## HIGHLY STRUCTURED HUMAN SOCIETIES

Social organization is based on possession and working of land. Tribal, clan and family territories are marked off ritually according to hierarchical rank which is in turn determined by the seniority of the different patrilineal groups and each territory may only be owned by men and women who mutually recognize each other as belonging to the same group. Within the strict framework fixed by custom, the individual has, however, a wide freedom. Thus the working of lands for raising cattle or crop cultivation may be assumed by "passing outsiders" who are not members of the property owner's group. The notion of "passing" can extend for years and, often, temporary nomadic groups settle permanently within the tribe which has accepted them. The three other founding principles of Aboriginal society in the north are absolute respect of family ties, exogamic unions and the observance of rituals. Marriage is considered as definitive and the preeminence of senior members undisputed, incest (even between distant cousins) being the worst offence. An individual's wealth and prestige must always be justified by an historic or moral antecedent.

Despite the influence of Whites, old cults still persist and young boys must go through numerous "mystical passages" during more or less secret ceremonies.

# 2/2

# NORTHERN AUSTRALIA

Aboriginal societies have a very spiritual conception of life and of man.

The strict respect of moral and religious rules (prohibition of crime and theft, exiling of offenders, recourse to magic, preservation of the environment) implies the existence of numerous taboos which mark daily life.

## RITES INHERITED FROM THE TIME OF DREAMS

The clans, which are patrilinear, share the land according to territorial partitions which go back into the mists of a time marked by the exploits of founding ancestors.

Hunting ground is, however, unlimited and hunters are authorized to hunt game right into the territory of another clan. The rightful owners of such land are, however, entitled to a part of the food hunted on their territory.

The influence of dreams, particularly those of a premonitory nature, is decisive. Based on the principle that any dream during sleep necessarily contains a part of reality, the Aborigines believe that counsel or orders come to them from the invisible world, so as to guide their everyday lives. Only wise men and sorcerers have received the gift of being able to communicate with the spirits and interpret their messages. Their sayings form the basis of an astonishing literature and numerous songs and dances. Tribal gatherings are occasions for playing and "living" the other reality of the parallel world. Despite the white man's policy of assimilation and the combative force of Christianity, these beliefs remain firmly rooted in a culture which goes back over ten thousand years.

Initiation rites also persist, such as circumcision and particularly subincision of young men, widespread practices in the Aboriginal world. Set aside from the women, novices must endure these difficult ordeals in order to prove that, by overcoming pain, they are able to surpass themselves in the interest of the group.

The ultimate goal of such ceremonies is to strengthen group spirit and bond the solidarity of a clan.

*Smearing his face with vegetal flour and clay means for this old Gunavidji that he is ready to communicate with the invisible spirits.*

◄

*On a hot afternoon,
a member of the Djuwali tribe
quenches his thirst with cool water from a stream on the Kimberley plateau.*

*The Lardils are partial to water lilies which they harvest after the rainy season.*
*According to tradition each picker must harvest the plants by beginning*
*in the centre and working his way out towards the ocean.*

◀

*At dusk, a small clan of Jirjironds settles down*
*to spend the night in the bush of the Cape York peninsula.*
*Their meal is made up of two large roasted lizards.*

*Collecting shellfish and mussels at low tide*
*is one of the activities reserved for women,*
*here on the island of Elcho.*

*Hunters stalking wallabies in the east of Arnhem Land.*
*The whitish termitaries contrast with a vegetation charred by sun and fires.*

*The technique employed by these Brinken goes back to prehistoric times.*
*The propulsion device enables the distance of the throw to be increased three-fold.*

*Stylized animals and stars*
*make up the usual motifs of ceremonial paintings.*

*These Miriwongs mime the celestial hunt of their founding ancestors.*
*Two musicians provide the rhythm for their dance.*
*The one on the left is blowing into a "didgeridoo", a long, hollow wooden tube*
*without a mouthpiece which produces raw and spellbinding sounds.*

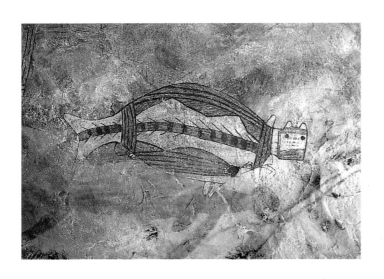

Arnhem Land offers a complete range of extremely old cave paintings. Highly-stylized, pencil-shaped human silhouettes adjoin animals drawn in "X-ray" style such as this Ummorduk barramunda.

The river Katherine ▶ flows through the heartland of a once sacred region for the Aborigines. It attracts numerous visitors both for the beauty of its landscapes and the cave paintings on its banks.

*A representation of the creation of the world*
*and its dividing up between three divine protectors,*
*according to stories from the legendary "time of dreams".*

# ABORIGINAL ART

Northern Australia houses the finest and oldest examples of Aboriginal art which, from its outset, has been closely linked with the "time of dreams". It is a living art in the sense that it perpetuates a primitive mythological and cultural substance, unsoiled by technological evolution and the advent of a new society.

## THE OLDEST ART ON EARTH

The oldest examples of Aboriginal art go back as far as 15,000 years, making it the oldest known artistic expression on earth. There are two specific characteristics which give it an original place in the framework of Oceanian art. Firstly, it is not an art reserved for specialists or recognized artists and each individual, including children, may create the work of his or her own choice. Secondly there is a generalized contrast between the poorness of the supports (bark, stones, shells) and the techniques used, together with the surprising degree of abstract expression of the themes represented. We must bear in mind that such an art emanates from primitive, nomadic tribes who for millenia have lived from gathering fruit and hunting and who therefore were forced to carry the least amount of things with them when on the move. Hence a clear distinction between artistic objects of modest size with utilitarian or ritual purposes (utensils, arms, statuettes, magic bones or wood) which they took with them and durable objects in their own right which they would leave on the inner walls of caves. The first have been handed down over successive generations and are the origin of present-day realisations that have remained practically unaltered. Besides their value as exceptional historical vestiges, wall paintings and engravings are often veritable masterpieces. Through study, it has been possible to establish four main phases in the evolution of Aboriginal art. The first dates from the Paleolithic period and is characterized by irregular and abstract engravings expressed by rough-drawn sketches associated with small holes. The following period used clearer linear outlines and included the first monochrome paintings, representing human beings and totemic animals. The Bronze Age saw the evolution of a more symbolic expression with geometrical figures and animal prints. Finally, artists produced naturalist, monumental and polychrome works which ritually associate the visible world of men and animals with the invisible world of the spirits, giving to Aboriginal art its final touch of timelessness and magic.

*Decor of a funeral post and totemic figure of the Tiwi, an ethnic group from the Bathurst and Melville islands, the production of which is much sought-after by lovers of primitive art.*

*The vast depression of Lake Eyre is 35 feet below sea level.*
*In parts it is taken over by a real desert, the surface of which is covered by salt.*

# 2 / 3

# CENTRAL AUSTRALIA

The vast zone made up by the desert expanses of Australia covers almost two thirds of the continent. It takes in most of the west of the country and the entire centre. Marked in the middle by the famous Ayres Rock, the largest monolith in the world and which is also the Aborigines' sacred mountain, it symbolizes perfectly the image which foreigners have of Australia. Large Aboriginal communities still go there. They live in far less structured societies than their northern counterparts but are perhaps closer to ancestral traditions. The best-known tribal confederations are the Bidjandjara, the Bindubi, the Walbiri and the Aranda.

## THE DESERT

The term desert covers in fact two distinct realities. Although the word is perfectly suited when applied to the west and the centre, it is more open to discussion when applied to the western subarid plateau. The deserts include the Great Western or Gibson Desert, the south Victoria Desert then the Nullarbor Plain (whose name is derived from the fact that there are no trees) and the Eastern or Simpson Desert extended, to the south, by the depression of Lake Eyre. These deserts encircle a central plateau called the "Red Centre" after the reddish colour of the rocks and which forms the oldest part of the Australian continent. The real deserts and the Red Centre are one of the most arid regions on earth, but, depending on which of the two zones you are in, the vegetation differs somewhat. In the deserts of sand or stone (the same as the erg or reg of the Sahara), the sparse vegetation, made up for the most part of thorny grasses hidden away in dried-up river beds, does its best in the face of an almost total absence of rain. The most desolate places are vast plains of small rocks (quartzite, jasper, chalcedony, red and purplish-blue in

colour), called gibbers from the Aboriginal word for stones.

On the immediate edge of the deserts, the desolate plains such as the Nullarbor or the Lake Eyre depression sometimes have rain which gives rise to a sparse vegetation of salsuginous grasses and thorny bushes.

The Red Centre, a large part of which resembles a succession of cliffs and eroded entablatures, is an area of scraggy scrub engendered by the occasional rains of January and February and which is called mallee scrub where eucalyptus trees predominate and mulga scrub where there are acacias.

## MEN ADAPTED TO DROUGHT

The need to survive in such a hostile environment has given rise to very specific types of societies. Each person in the group knows and communicates bearings in relation to relief, sun, stars, hunting and stalking techniques. Since survival is impossible outside a group context, the sense of tribe is very strong. The individual exists only via and for the clan. A community feeling governs every aspect of daily life, and the clan will assume charge of the wife or children of those who are sick or have died. The birthrate is high as the children will have to look after their parents once they become old. Scarcity of water and variety of species for food have made men adapt physically and spiritually to their environment. Everyone carries with them a mental calendar which enables them to read, "instinctively" in the eyes of others, things such as the wind, heat, cold or the presence of vegetation or animals.

In these places where practically no edible plant grows apart from a few dried-up species, the Aborigines have a particularly strong dentition and strong jaws which enable them to chew even the hardest grains.

*A group of shamans belonging to the Gadudjara,
the Bidandjara and the Aranda prepares to celebrate a "corroboree"
during which the ritual of circumcision will be carried out.
The conical hats are made of bark attached by human hair.*

*Synthetic paint and cotton*
*are increasingly replacing traditional pigments and flock.*

*A typical Red centre landscape, here to the south of Alice Springs.*

*Highly-eroded reliefs are scattered in vast, arid stretches of sand and rocks covered by sparse scrub.*

In these burnt and barren stretches where rare animals scurry off at the slightest hint of danger, hunters carry long-distance arms, such as boomerangs and propulsion devices with which they can reach prey that is too fast for them to hunt down. Vital elements for survival, game and water have been assimilated into myths as well as the social and moral order of the tribes. They form part of the bonds with which Aborigines have defined ritual inter-relationships. Members of each family and clan are therefore linked to a totemic animal which they must not kill, except in cases of extreme necessity and only then after a long expiatory ceremony. On the other hand, the animal, which is regarded as the terrestrial representation of an invisible being from the "time of dreams", is supposed to watch over his human "brothers" whose existence is ensured by the sacrifice, freely granted by the animals themselves, of certain amongst them. Besides giving a rich spiritual dimension to life in the desert, such a conception has the advantage of proposing an efficient and ecological method for preserving animal life and consequently a source of food. The periods of relative abundance are an opportunity for tribes to come together at occasions which are called corroboree. The clans meet to eat, sing, dance to the sound of the didgeridoo (a sort of large, long wooden flute), to listen to epic, marvellous tales that go back into the mists of time, and organize marriages. But in particular, the corroborees are the moment when initiation ceremonies are carried out and religious mysteries celebrated, as they have been over the millenia amongst Aborigines.

*Contrary to a widespread but false belief,*
*the hunting boomerang used by these two Arandas*
*does not come back to its thrower.*
*Another type of fighting boomerang exists,*
*whose form imitates the bent claw of the kangeroo.*

*Once adorned in accordance with tradition, and acting on behalf of tribal chiefs, the shamans perform a dance of "presentation" to the spirits around a totem pole.*

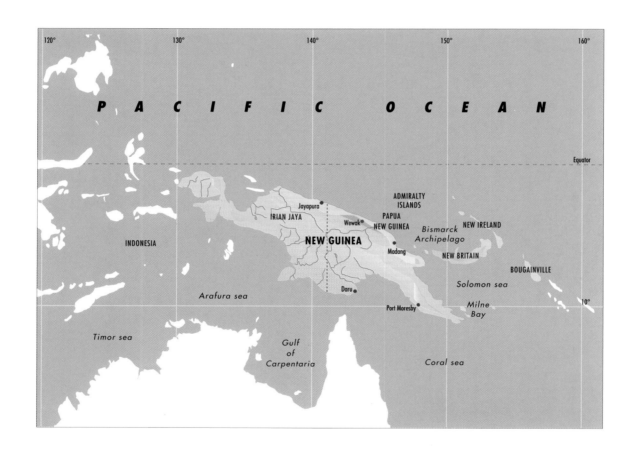

PACIFIC OCEAN

Equator

INDONESIA

IRIAN JAYA

Jayapura

ADMIRALTY
ISLANDS

PAPUA
Wewak NEW GUINEA

NEW GUINEA

Bismarck
Archipelago

NEW IRELAND

Madang

NEW BRITAIN

BOUGAINVILLE

Solomon sea

Daru

Arafura sea

Milne
Bay

10°

Port Moresby

Timor sea

Gulf
of
Carpentaria

Coral sea

# 3
## 1

# NEW GUINEA

With a surface area of 884,000 km², New Guinea is the second largest island in the world after Greenland. Politically it is divided into two more or less equal parts, Irian Jaya to the west which belongs to Indonesia and the independent Papua New Guinea which is part of the British Commonwealth. Numerous archipelagoes are also attached to the island and administered by Irian Jaya or Papua New Guinea according to their geographical situation. Those belonging to the latter, traditionally called Papuan archipelagoes (although in fact inhabited by Melanesians) constitute a separate entity and will be dealt with in the chapter on Melanesia.

## AN ISLAND THAT AROSE FROM THE VIOLENT COLLISION OF CRUSTAL PLATES

New Guinea arose from the collision between the Indo-Australian plate and the plate of the Philippines sea to the north and the Pacific to the east. Its southern part is a vast continental shelf directly attached to the Australian shield of which it is part. It is a stable zone, entirely covered with several superimposed layers of detrital deposits whose accumulation continued from the Jurrasic to the Quaternary period. Separated from this shelf by the Lagaip fault, the large central mountainous range constitutes the unstable edge of the Australian shield, continually acted upon by orogenic forces. In the eastern part of the island, it is bordered to the south by a complex structure of low sedimentary mountains. It is essentially made up of limestone formations from the Jurassic and the Cretaceous periods with inclusions of eruptive rocks (granites, syenites, diorites) which have accumulated on the ancient metamorphic substratum (gneiss, green schists). The whole zone underwent a violent uplift at the end of the Cretaceous period. There then followed an extremely complex series of new upheavals and interconnections between deep trenches. Finally in the Upper Miocene era began the major orogenic phase of the central range. The uplift of the secondary range to the north took place during the Mid- and Upper Pliocene periods over a zone of faults marking an area of subduction. Finally in the Quaternary, powerful faults brought about the delta formations of the major rivers.

## IMPRESSIVE MOUNTAIN MASSES AND PUTRID SWAMPS

New Guinea offers a double aspect; mountainous in its northern part, low and swampy to the south. Between the two, a remarkable mountain barrier, fragmented and high in altitude (culminating in the Puncak Jaya peak, 16,500 feet in Irian), forms a backbone which is difficult to traverse and stretches from one end of the island (Cenderawasih or Vogelkop) to the Huon peninsula.
The mountain range has a massive and linear structure in its western part where it is highest. The Puncak Jaya culminates in a compact mountainous mass which is never less than 13,000 feet in height. The eastern part of the range is not as high (Mount Wilhelm is, however, 14,800 feet in height) with a mean altitude of 11,500 feet and a much more complex morphology. Instead of overlooking the

alluvion plains to the south, as in Irian Jaya, the central range splits into a series of lower secondary mountains that make up a sort of gigantic plateau before the southern plains. As a result of intense tectonic activity, the range is divided into several blocks (Maoke Mounts, the Victor Emmanuel Range, the Bismarck and Owen Stanley Mounts). The north and south sides are notched by deep valleys. To the north of the central range, depressions, oriented along the central axis, have created several parallel ranges (the Tamrau and Van Rees Mounts, the Adelbert, Finisterre, Saruwaged and Torricelli Ranges), marked out by volcanoes, many of which are active. They belong to the long line of volcanoes situated directly over the large fracture that goes as far as New Britain. Between the coastal mountains and the central range, major rivers (Mamberamo, Sepik, Ramu) have etched wide furrows which, when they

approach the sea, are transformed into vast, swampy plains. The south of New Guinea is an immense stretch of alluvial plains, covered with unhealthy, parasite-ridden swamps, including malaria-bearing mosquitoes. Orogenic movements have brought about a slight tilting in the island substratum towards the west. One of the consequences of this is that the Irian Jaya plains are lower than their eastern counterparts. After their descent from the central mountains, numerous fast-flowing rivers (Lorentz, Pulau, Digul, Kanuwe, Kikori, Aramia, Purari and above all the Fly which measures 1,100 km) meander across them. Flat and low, the coast is broken up by wide estuaries littered with unstable, alluvial islands.

◄

*The impressive central range of New Guinea is notched by numerous rivers. The terrential waters spill out into deep, narrow valleys whose walls are lined with thick tropical vegetation.*

## AN EQUITORIAL CLIMATE

Situated just below the Equator, the island of New Guinea has an equitorial climate marked by high temperatures (mean 28°C) and a narrow annual temperature range. Near to the intertropical convergence zone, the island is subject to rains throughout the year with an annual rainfall of several metres. They are more abundant from December to April, when the monsoon winds blow from the north-west. From May to November, the south-east trade winds gain the upper hand and subject the island to marine influences. The characteristics of this equatorial climate vary according to the disposition and the height of the relief. Windward slopes receive much more rain than leeward ones, creating a significant difference in rain distribution which can be anything up to four-fold (1500 to 6000 mm of rain per year). With the exception of the south-east of the island, near to Australia which has a drier climate, total annual rainfall in the low coastal areas and the swampy plains reaches 2000 mm of water. Above 5,000 feet in altitude, there is an equatorial mountain climate without any seasonal variations in temperature but with considerable daytime variations. Temperatures drop approximately one degree every 3,300 feet. Between 5,000 and 8,200 feet they go from 13°C in the morning to 18°C in the afternoon before dropping again in the evening. Above 8,200 feet, frequent night frosts occur in the mountains but certain interior high plains which are sheltered from the wind enjoy a temperate climate with temperatures varying between 10°C and 15°C. Over 9,800 feet the climate becomes cold. Summits over 14,800 feet are covered in perpetual snow and have small glaciers.

The regular and abundant nature of rainfall has given rise to an orographical network which the central range, a natural watershed, distributes evenly on both slopes. The numerous rivers have irregular courses due to the uneven terrain and, in their upper breaches are torrent-like and raging to become wider as they muddily meander across the plains.

## DENSE FORESTS, BIRDS, REPTILES AND INSECTS

Flora is determined by the climate and alters as the latter changes. The forest is everywhere dominant. Three zones of vegetation may be noted. The coastal zones feature mangroves with 36 different vegetable species indexed, including bruguieres and rhizophora. Then coconut trees, pandanus (screw pine) and ironwood trees herald the swampy plains and lowlands which, up to 3,300 feet are covered by a thick, damp equatorial forest which occasionally gives way to tall, savanna grasses. Species are relatively varied

with in particular the sago palm which supplies one of the basic foods for New Guineans, and high-boled trees (eucalyptus, melaleuca, kauri, klinki). The less rainy regions of the south-east have a grassy savanna vegetation (dominated by the kumai), scattered with albizzias, myristicas and acacias. Between 3,300 feet and 9,800 feet is the high tropical forest, characterized by vast zones of southern conifer, oak and beech growing side by side, recalling those of Tasmania or New Zealand. The dense undergrowth generally has several stages of vegetation with

*Game is rare and yet hunting remains the main means of subsistence for populations living in the most remote part of the world, central Irian Jaya.*

◀ *The dispersion of villages in the heart of the forest, here on the northern slopes of the Jayawijaya mounts, has protected whole areas from contact with the modern world, thereby preserving local cultures.*

numerous lianas, ferns, mosses, epiphytes and orchids of which over 2,770 varieties have been indexed. Above 9,800 feet, on the mountainous slopes which are often enveloped in fog, comes the rhododendron zone which forms the transition between the sparse, stunted forest (up to over 860 species, almost 300 of which are indigenous. The best known are the 36 varieties of paradise birds with their multi-coloured plumage and large running-birds such as the cassowary which have lost the use of their wings since, at the moment of separation from Gondwana, there

11,500 feet) and the high-mountain pastures (over 12,500 feet).

New Guinea has a rich fauna, but species are unequally represented and distributed. The reason for this lies in the geographical position of the island between Asia and Australia. There are few mammals. Some 200 species have been indexed, 93 of which are indigenous, of which 43 are monotremes, including echidna, cuscus, the oppossum, the tree-dwelling kangaroo, the wallaby and 52 bats and rodents.

The region is exceptionally rich in bird life with were no predators present. There are also numerous parrots (42 species), honey-eating birds (59 species), bower-birds or ortolans, eagles and kingfishers. Reptiles are also well represented with over 100 species of snakes, over 200 lizards, crocodiles and tortoises. There are also some 200 species of amphibians. New Guinea is a hive for insects. It has been estimated that there are between 50,000 and 100,000 species, including 5,000 for butterflies alone, extremely prized by collectors.

# THE PAPUANS

The term Papuans was given by the Portuguese De Menses who named New Guinea ilhas dos Papuas from the Malay term papuwah ("fuzzy") after the natives' hair. The word has been applied for the sake of simplicity to cover all New

*One of the bridges spanning the torrents of the Tifalmin region in the Victor Emmanuel Range in western Papua New Guinea.*

Guineans but in fact englobes an extremely complex reality marked by the dispersion and particular nature of the innumerable ethnic and linguistic groups. Thousands of tribes have been indexed, as well as over 1,000 main languages, themselves subdivided into dialects which, in turn, have local idioms. The further research goes, the more complex the situation becomes. It is impossible to draw up an ethnological picture of New Guinea. At best we can outline a few major ethnic and linguistic zones with a common "culture". The most important ethnic groups are, for Irian Jaya, the Biaki, the Dani, the Yali (or Jale), the Kapauku, the Ngalum, the Enarotali and the Asmat, and for Papua New Guinea, the Abelam, the Washkuk, the Iatmul, the Maring, the Hagen, the Chimbu, the Medlpa, the Huli and the Mendi.

All village communities share a few common socio-cultural characteristics. There is little hierarchical structure, insofar as, during the council meetings, the different chiefs are placed on the same egalitarian footing. A "big chief" is sometimes appointed when he has to represent a large tribal group during a ceremony or with the authorities. His status and prestige, and hence his power, are linked to the possession of land and what goes with it, crops and livestock (essentially pigs). To the territory is linked the notion of clan, lineage or cognate family ties.

These land rights are hereditary via consanguinity in lineal descent, either on the father's or the mother's side. They may, however, also be acquired by marriage or various alliances. The close family forms the basic social cell, i.e. restricted to relatives in immediate ascending or descending line. Each family is integrated into a clan, the total clans forming a tribe, linked by a number of common mythical ancestors. Communities are often small, most of them with a maximum of 500.

Large tribal confederations which have woven close bonds of exchange between their various component parts, such as the Dani of Irian Jaya or the Medlpa of Papua New Guinea, count, however, respectively 250,000 and 100,000 individual members.

There is absolute ritual separation between men and women and each community is compelled to perform specific daily tasks (the men work and plant the gardens, the women harvest) and have ceremonies from which the other is excluded. Thus the entrance to the "large men's houses" where only initiated men may enter is strictly forbidden to women.

The practice of inter-clan and inter-tribal exchanges goes back to the most ancient times. Their objective is to designate a special zone where tribes, that have become kin as a result of the ritual exchange of presents, no longer fight between themselves.

Bartering farm produce (tubers, bananas, coconuts, pigs, chickens) is widespread even if, nowadays, competition with modern goods (clothes, transistor radios) is beginning to be felt.

*Men from mountain tribes, here a Jale and two Kurelu both wear a protective penile cover made from a hollowed-out colocynth. Its name varies from one ethnic group to the next but everyone can understand it by its generic term "koteka".*

*T*he world as we know it today did not need to be created, as it had existed since the dawn of time. It was eternal and unchanging. The sky was on high and knew the winds and the clouds. It allowed rain to fall onto the earth and the Ocean which were below. The tides stirred the Ocean and waves rolled over its surface. Only the earth had a slightly different consistency. It was a mass of brownish, liquid mud flowing ceaselessly into itself, for which reason it was unable to construct or maintain the least relief. At that time there were no living or mortal creatures. The world was dominated by the original gods, the wagan. They would frequently come together to talk and chew betel. Amongst them were two brothers whose prestige was incomparable, being superior in strength and magic to all the others. Each time that someone needed a reliable opinion or a new idea, it was to them that questions were put. They were called Kava'mbuangga and Wolindambwi. Although they were brothers, they were not alike. The first was peaceful and spent his time weaving matting and baskets. The second was warlike and made fearsome arms. And yet Kava'mbuangga had one advantage. He was master of the invisible world. Sometimes he shared its secrets with his brother. Both could easily pass from the visible world to the invisible one, even appear at one and the same time in both. Death only existed in a virtual way, in a latent state. It had been decided that as long as a wagan did not invoke it on someone's head, it would not manifest itself. One day, as Kava'mbuangga was practising some magic tricks, he caused two new beings to appear by chance, one of which flew away into the skies and the other plunged into the seas. He had unintentionally created the first bird and the first fish. He decided to continue with his creation and first of all invented everything that lived in the air and in the water. Then he turned towards the earth. He placed his foot in the mud which solidified as soon as he had done so. The water it contained left it and combined to form the streams and rivers. Firm land could then be raised and the mountains appeared above the plains. He then had to people them with living creatures, just as he had done so with the skies and the Ocean. Kava'mbuangga began to spit his betel on the ground. Then, with his foot, he carefully crushed the reddish spit. Each time that the wagan raised his foot, a creature was born in the imprint. Kava'mbuagga's work lasted a long time. When he had finished, he looked at his work. Everything that exists on earth, plants, animals and men, had appeared. He brought them to life by breathing over them and gave them the ability to reproduce. He noted that the plants and animals multiplied much faster than men. Out of a sense of equity, he limited their lifespan by invoking death on the head of the first two species. He believed that each had the right to live and that plants and animals, once they had reached their alloted span, should die and disappear into the earth so as to leave room for their own descendants and above all should not stifle humanity. The wagan taught the different living creatures on earth to adapt as best as possible to their environment. They adorned the birds that lived at the top of trees where it was difficult to reach them, with iridescent colours. He showed the snakes how to hide in the bushes. He gave the wild hog sharp tusks and the cuscus which was sensitive to the cold a warm fur. Kava'mbuangga and Wolindambwi paid particular attention to human beings. The former gave them intelligence and the gift of agriculture, the latter aggressiveness and a war-faring instinct. Kava'mbuangga taught them how to build villages. He charged them to separate the women whose menstruations periodically made them impure, from initiated males. The latter had to live together in the house of the warriors. The wagan allowed them to communicate with him. For this he gave them sacred drums and flutes as well as statues symbolizing the invisible forces, which enabled them to communicate with the spirits. He ordered them to place all these objects in the house of the warriors. No woman would be allowed to enter under pain of death. All the men had already gone inside when Wolindambwi arrived, furious at not having been associated with this decision. Out of rage, he set fire to the ritual house and destroyed its occupants. In so doing, he had invoked death upon them. When his anger had subsided, Wolindambwi asked his brother for forgiveness and built a new house. But death did not wish to return its preys and there were no more men to inhabit the great house. The souls of those who had

# The legend of Kava'mbuangga

*Characteristic of the New Guinean world marked by violence and magic, the following legend is part of the Iatmul cosmogony, an ethnic group from the mid-Sepik region.*

perished in the fire demanded justice and complained that their fate was different from that of the women, who were still immortal. So as to re-establish equality between humans, Kava'mbuangga granted them more magical powers than their husbands as compensation. Since then, no human being can escape death, and women have stronger magic than men. But the wagan did not want men to be subjected to the same law as the other creatures and disappear into the ground. He therefore gave them the possibility, once dead, of living again in the invisible world of which he was the master.

Thus it was that the ghosts appeared which intervene in everyday life. Certain have good intentions, for they are the ancestors of clans and help the living. Others are full of evil intentions and hound them by imparting disease and evil spells. In order to complete his work, Kava'mbuagga spat twice more onto the ground. He crushed the betel stains with his foot. From the spit came the kargwa (sorcerers) who were charged with being the intermediaries between the visible and the invisible worlds. From the second arose the windjimbu (tree spirits) who were charged with watching over the forest. Henceforth humanity could develop and take possession of the earth which is the permanent stage for the subtle play between magic and nature.

*An Asmat warrior practising his bow and arrow
on the vast muddy beach bordering the Arafura sea,
not far from the Dolak peninsula.*

Irian Jaya constitutes the western half of New Guinea with a surface area of 395,000 km², to which various island dependencies must be added including the Schouten islands (Biak and Yapen), Waigeo, Misool, Kai (or Ewab), Tanimbar and Aru, covering an area of 27,000 km².

## THE IMPOSSIBLE ENCOUNTER BETWEEN PAPUANS AND WHITES

When consulting recent maps of Irian Jaya, even the most recent and most accurate, we perceive "white zones" which correspond to regions that are still badly known or which have simply not yet been penetrated by outsiders. It is the least explored region on earth. There are doubtless small tribes which have lived without the least contact with white people.

Irian Jaya, whose capital is Jayapura, has officially belonged to the Republic of Indonesia since 1963. New Guinea was recognized by Portuguese navigators at the beginning of the 16th Century, then by the Dutch Schouten, Lemaire and Carstensz during the following century, before falling into oblivion. In 1848, and amidst general indifference, Holland annexed the western part of the island and drove out the small British contingent that had settled there some years earlier. Contacts with the rare coastal populations were very limited as the natives fled at the sight of the Whites. Subsequently, Irian Jaya did not attract many explorers before the middle of the 19th Century. Covered by impenetrable forests, considered as the devil's land on account of the reputation of its belligerent inhabitants, the province was visited from 1840 onwards by a few scientists and especially by Dutch, British and German traffickers attracted by precious wood and copra. Relationships with natives, unavoidable on account of the need for labour, were always brutal. Europeans killed Papuans without compunction whom they did not regard as human beings and reduced the others to slavery. All the ethnic groups of Irian Jaya were divided by ceaseless warfare and were cannibalistic and headhunters. They had no advanced technique and led a prehistoric life. They were, however, relatively spared from European colonization, as most of

# 3/2

# IRIAN JAYA
## A PROVINCE OUT OF THE MISTS OF TIME

them were protected by the inaccessible forests and mountains, which explains the exceptional preservation of local traditions. Only the missionaries ventured inland, but conversions were few and far between. Tribes from the coastal areas and the plains were, on the other hand, unable to defend themselves and were pitilessly subjugated. This shameful system of slavery lasted into the 20th Century, when the Dutch had to give way to the Indonesians in 1963. This changed nothing for the native populations who have since been submitted to the military authority of Jakarta and its lack of regard for human rights.

## ETHNIC GROUPS HARDLY EMERGED FROM THE STONE AGE

In its dense forests and high mountains, Irian Jaya houses extremely primitive ethnic groups, the conditions of whose existence are reminiscent of the Neolithic age. These direct descendants of the first populations of the island number approximately 970,000, or 60% of the 1,630,000 inhabitants of the province. Although tribal wars are generally on the decrease, they are still current practice. The valley of Baliem, the mountains of Angguruk and Kono, the Asmat marshes and high valleys of Oksibil were the theatre of ceaseless fighting, albeit often limited and short in duration. An atmosphere of insidious warfare still lingers and the periods of truce, sometimes linked to the seasons, mark native life. Social groups are small in size (less than 400 members) and are constituted into "mini-republics", extremely attached to traditions and deeply egalitarian. Birth does not confer any chiefdom or important mark of distinction. The system is based on an individual aggressiveness by means of which the warrior acquires prestige and power, thus land and pigs, by his prowess in combat. Marriages, inter-clan alliances, ceremonial exchanges, yam and taro competitions enable rival groups to be made up which, for limited periods, give over to popular "heroes" who remain at their head for as long as their prestige remains untarnished.

But the situation never lasts very long. This goes for the populations in the interior who continue to have only restricted relations with the outside

*The southern half of Irian Jaya*
*is a vast extent of swampy plains covered by hostile forests.*
*Wide, muddy rivers listlessly flow towards the south, as here the Mappi.*

world. As for the others who live in "modern" regions, their status is hardly enviable as they have been literally phagocytized by the hundreds of thousands of settlers that Jakarta sends to Irian. For the last five years alone, 750,000 Indonesians, mostly Javanese, have come to settle. Throughout the province, major commercial interests such as the timber industry (often entrusted to the Japanese) and oil fields have worked in the same direction as the united efforts of Indonesian Islam and the fervent Christianism of the missionaries, all of which are to the detriment of New Guinean tribes. In 1995, several of them were displaced by force, and certain groups wiped out, without the international community showing undue care. Most of the ethnic groups have entered into a state of lethargy in the face of a world which they do not understand and against which they have no way of resisting. The work of mutilation carried out by certain missionaries in Irian Jaya has reached a level unheard of in the Pacific, putting a full stop to exceptional primitive cultures. Little concerned by what is going on around them, not even by the two world wars which nevertheless affected New Guinea, the Irian inhabitants have never experienced any general independence movements, as in other parts of Oceania. Just a single sporadic rebellion has stirred up the east of the province since the mid sixties, but without much result in spite of the aid which is sometimes given by the neighbouring state of Papua New Guinea. Exiled in the Benin, a revolutionary government was set up in 1971. After the success of the separatist organization Papua Merdeka in 1977 and the Indonesian army's bloody counter-offensive, peace was signed in 1980. Since then, Irian Jaya Papuans have passively looked on as others have run their future for them. It seems difficult to ask people who have just emerged from the Stone Age to enter the 20th Century.

*Ancestral techniques have not varied since the Neolithic era.*
*The long dugout canoes made from tree trunks*
*are propelled by boat-hooks and not paddles.*
*Magical figures, whose role is to protect those in the boat,*
*are carved onto the prow using fire-hardened sticks.*

*As a sign of mourning for a man of their family,*
*women must respect a terrible ritual that comes from the mists of time;*
*they cut off the phalanges of their fingers, but leave that of the thumb which is sacred.*

*Sweet potatoes and various rhizomes are steamed on a bed of white-hot stones*
*which are then covered with wet grasses.*

*Women, belonging to the Ekagi ethnic group,*
*draw water from a muddy backwater fed by a river*
*coming down from the Sudirman mounts.*

*The most sought-after adornments
mix shells with "cuscus" furs
and cassowary and cockatoo feathers.
A hole pierced in the nasal cavity
is for placing bird-quills
or large white two-sided seashells.*

◄

*An adoption ceremony
at the Baintambor Asmats during
which the community will adopt members
of the neighbouring Tjitjak ethnic group.*

*The majority of the New Guinean territory
is covered by impenetrable forest.
Heat and high ambient humidity give rise
to thick tropical vegetation.*

Since 1975, Papua New Guinea is an independent state within the British Commonwealth. Its capital is Port Moresby. Territorial waters cover a surface area of 3,210,000 km² and land surface area is 462,000 km², including 58,000 km² of various archipelagoes (Bismarck, Louisiade, western Solomon), which will be dealt with in Chapter 5 on Melanesia of which they are culturally and ethnologically a part.

## A LAND OF VIOLENCE

The Portuguese Antonio de Abreu was the first to set foot on the main island of New Guinea in 1512. Other Iberian navigators followed, including Iñigo Ortiz de Retes who, on seeing black-skinned natives like the ones in Africa, decided to call the land New Guinea.

### FOUGHT OVER BY THE MAJOR POWERS

At the beginning of the 16ᵗʰ Century, Madrid seemed scarcely interested in New Guinea. The Dutch took advantage and annexed the western part of the island, whilst the British and Australians settled in the east. So as to avoid a conflict between the two European powers, a border was drawn up in 1828 to separate Papua New Guinea from its western neighbour, present-day Irian Jaya attached to Indonesia but which was, at the time, under Dutch control. Shortly afterwards, other Europeans, Germans, began to settle in the eastern part of the island. The British and Australians on one side, and the Germans on the other, began to annex small territories. In the last third of the 19ᵗʰ Century, German ambitions in the northern half of Papua New Guinea became more apparent, in particular with the installation of the powerful Hernsheim company in 1873. Clearly worried, in 1883, Queensland Australians launched a vast propaganda and emigration operation whose aim was to occupy the maximum amount of territory as a counter to German intentions. Under pressure from Berlin, London disappproved of this under-taking, whilst at the same time placing the south of the island under the British protectorate. Germany reacted swiftly and annexed several archipelagoes, including the Bismarck archipe-lago, placing them under protectorate like the

# 3 / 3

# PAPUA NEW GUINEA

eastern coasts. German-British rivalry grew dan-gerously. After both recognizing the rights of Holland over the western part of New Guinea, the two rival powers signed, however, a convention the following year recognizing German rights over the Bismarck archipelago and the northern part of the island which became known as Kaiser Wilhelmsland, and Anglo-Australian rights over the southern part. In 1888 this protectorate became a British colony under the name of Papua New Guinea before being integrated into the Australian Commonwealth in 1906. At the begin-ning of the First World War the Australians took advantage of German commitments in Europe and landed in northern New Guinea which the League of Nations placed under their trust in 1921.

Although the territory was thereby united, peace did not follow. In 1942, the Japanese occupied most of the eastern archipelagoes and northern coasts. The island was once again subjected to major battles until reconquered by the Allies in 1944-45. After the League of Nations had recon-firmed the Australian mandate over the former German possessions, the two parts of the coutry were reunited into a single state which, in 1949, became known as Papua New Guinea.

### THE PAY-BACK SYSTEM

Papua New Guinea is a violent country, whether it be in the streets of Port Moresby or the dark forests of the interior. As far back as human memory goes, particularly through oral traditions, warfare for possession of land, women or pigs was part of the daily landscape. It is a sacred honour for men to take part in a battle defending the clan or the tribe. The influence of the Whites and the efforts of various local governments have succeeded in eradicating ritual war from "civilised" zones, but the least incident between tribes degenerates into a brutal conflict, particularly in the remote villages. The conflicts cannot in fact stop since tribal rules stipulate that each wrong must be righted by vengeance in blood. This tradi-tion is known by the pidgin term pay back. Peace is measured by the varying lengths of time between two conflicts. Amongst the methods used to desacralise war and channel violence, the

*This Huli from the region of Tari,*
*in the low mountains of the south-west,*
*is wearing a headdress made from his wife's hair.*
*So as not to damage his precious head gear during the night,*
*he sleeps on a wooden head-rest.*

*A small hamlet situated in the high valley of the Jimmi,*
*in the foothills of the Bismark Mounts Range.*

system invented by the Australians when they administered the country is the one that still works the best. They succeeded in persuading the chiefs of the main tribal confederations in the most troubled area (a vast zone stretching from Laiagam and Wabag to Bayer, Hagen and Minj) that blood could be replaced by objects of value, such as feathers from rare birds, sea-shells, pigs, sacred yams or money. Use of this material pay back system spread gradually throughout the country from the 30's onwards. Since then, after exchanging mutual "ambassadors", enemies agree to finding a place where the pay back ritual may take place. On the agreed day, each clan, led by its big man or ceremonial chief, arrives in its finest array to compete with its opponents in events called sing sing, moka or tee. After impressive verbal defiance, simulated combats and parades, the jurys formed by mutually-agreed chiefs, classify the participants in an order which will determine the gifts given as compensation to each clan. Face is saved for everyone and those who have been defeated one day know that they have the possibility of taking their revenge in a peaceful way. This system has not, however, completely supplanted inter-ethnic conflicts. The last to date was in 1991 and caused much bloodshed in the central mountains, despite the intervention of the authorities. Nevertheless, the present pay back system has become one of the basic customary rules. Each year a major show is even put on in the central mountains, either in Hagen or Goroka, for foreign tourists to marvel at the spectacle of thousands of Papuans in magnificent attire.

*The inhabitants of the mid-Sepik*
*are reputed to have the most elegant adornments in the north.*
*The harmonious arrangement of sea-shells, plants, feathers and painting*
*of these Washkuk and Hunstein seem to confirm such a reputation.*

*Villagers from the region of Malewai make their way back to the lakeside*
*after a ceremony to drown bad spirits in the middle of a lake.*

# A MOST SOUGHT-AFTER PRIMITIVE ART

More than in Irian Jaya, Papua New Guinea offers an astonishing artistic variety. Artists have created very different styles and continue to produce remarkable works, despite an inevitable deterioration as a result of widespread commercialization. Museums and private collectors from all over the world haggle, sometimes for vast amounts of money, over objects which, at the outset, were in no way destined for such a fate. Like most primitive arts, New Guinean art has a ritual and magical vocation linked originally to funeral rites. Relations with foregone ancestors, communication with the invisible world, blessing or curse for whoever possesses the object, such are some of the initial objectives which are, however, beginning to be forgotten as the modern world encroaches.

There are several stylistic zones in Papua New Guinea. The two most characteristic ones, and therefore the most sought-after, are from mid- and low-Sepik and the Gulf of Huon, the former being the richest throughout Oceania. Amongst others, specialists distinguish Abelam, Iatmul, Korewori, Keram, Lagoon, Maprik, Mundugumor, Murik, Ramu, Tchambouli, Tshuosh and Washkuh styles. Although each is different and regardless of the support chosen (thread-like votive statues, decorated bark, head-rests, drums, flutes and especially remarkable masks), they all seek to produce an aesthetic effect. Use of vivid colours (red, yellow, white, blue, black) and sea-shells which voluntarily "complicate" the main theme so as to induce an effort of reflection within the onlooker and the studied harmony of curved forms combine to woo the eye before the mind. The ritual function of the work of art has lost its primary importance in favour of the aesthetic priority of form.

With less emphasis on aesthetic effects, artistic expression in the Gulf of Huon is a very different. It specializes in wood carving which has reached perfection in the highly stylized representation of an omnipresent bestiary.

The natives are seafarers for whom their dugout canoes have always represented the basic tool of their trade. There is therefore nothing surprising in the fact that it is the prows, treated like personified beings, which offer the most refined artistic examples. Effigies of crocodiles, birds or fish are supposed to attract the protection of these totemic animals for the boat crew. Human representations on the other hand, squat and heavy,

*Frieze of "nggwalndu", effigies of foregone ancestors consulted by clan chiefs before adopting any important decision relating to the community, painted on the bark faáade of an Abelem "haus tambaran" (house of the spirits) in the region of Maprik.*

are often stereotyped and far removed from the elegance of the former. With their heads sunk into their shoulders, their massive torsos and short, half-bent legs give them a heavy and ungraceful appearance. They are not carved to attract but to link the world of the living with that of the dead.

*A medicine man of a Chimbu tribe carries out a chant atop a ritual mast*
*so as to neutralize evil influences threatening the village.*

*The dance of the famous "mud men" in the region of Goroka.*
*This tradition seems to originate from the village of Kiminiwi.*
*Besieged by enemies and on the point of giving in,*
*the inhabitants are supposed to have made themselves up as ghosts,*
*thereby putting their terrorized assailants to flight.*

*A woman from the Tipuka clan,*
*with her face covered by a "spider-mask".*
*The red symbolizes fertility.*

◀

*The "sing sing", called "moga"*
*by the highland Medlpa (here near to Banz),*
*periodically bring together tribes*
*from the same region.*
*The ceremonial exchanges which take place*
*between the clans, often foes by tradition,*
*ensure a relative peace*
*within these fierce communities.*

The "sing sing" are the opportunity for warriors, here the Kawelka,
to compete with each other during the prestige parades.
They sing of the valourous deeds of their respective clans and vie for the finest adornments.

*The black paint used to make up the men is intended to put fear into the enemy.*
*It is often used in combination with the white tinting (generally derived from sago flour) of the beard,*
*evoking the ancestral wisdom of which men are the trustees.*

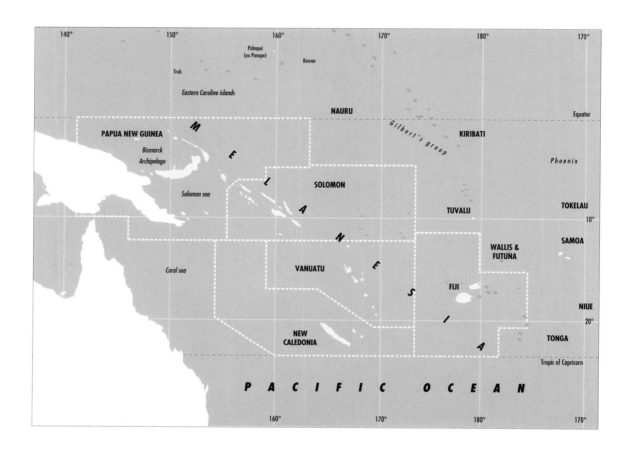

# 4

## 1

# MELANESIA

$M$elanesia, or "black islands" derives its name from the colour of the skin of its inhabitants (from the Greek *melas* "black" and *nesos* "island") who live on the large islands and archipelagoes of the western Pacific, south of the Equator, on four island groups, three of which are independent states: the Solomon Islands, Vanuatu and the Fiji Islands and the fourth of which is the French overseas territory of New Caledonia. Geographers and geologists have a wider conception of Melanesia than ethnologists. They prefer to talk of a Melanesian zone which they call marginal Oceania, as opposed to Oceania itself, represented by Micronesia and Polynesia. Within marginal Oceania, they distinguish two zones: the internal and external Melanesian belts. The first includes the Louisiade archipelago (belonging to Papua New Guinea), New Caledonia and New Zealand. The external belt includes the Bismarck archipelago, the Solomons, Vanuatu, Fiji and Tonga.

## THE FRAGMENTED LIMITS OF THE AUSTRALIAN SHIELD

It is thought that the internal Melanesian belt was only formed during the Jurassic period, whereas its external counterpart appeared at the end of the Cretaceous and during the Tertiary. As with most of Oceania, its formation was made possible by the presence of a high underwater rise, often referred to as the Darwin fold, which, from the Mesozoic period, stretched for over 40 million km² in the western and central Pacific. Throughout the whole of the Mesozoic period, the Darwin fold was subjected to a continual succession of uplifts before undergoing an intense volcanic phase, with lava flows emerging in massive proportions through the faults in the ocean plate, brought about by strong shear movements. Many Oceanian archipelagoes, particularly in Melanesia, were formed at this time. Later, during the Cenozoic period, a general subsidence engulfed most of these eruptive formations which were already surrounded by atolls. Subsequent uplifting and immersion made constant and profound modifications in the appearance of the Melanesian archipelagoes. Although, for the most part, they have a very similar geological origin and structure, the aspect of the emerged part is very different and often unique in its type, thus making it impossible to define any "typical" Melanesian archipelago.

## A WET TROPICAL CLIMATE

Melanesia is situated in the intertropical zone between the Equator and the Tropic of Capricorn. The climate is warm and rainy, with abundant rainfalls in the mountainous Solomon islands, Vanuatu and New Caledonia, with a net disproportion between the drier western slopes, protected from the trade winds by the mountains (mean annual fall 2,000mm) and the eastern slopes which are exposed to the winds and can receive up to 7,500mm of rain per year, and in extreme cases 10,000mm, as on the east coast of Guadalcanal in the Solomon islands. Vegetation is particularly luxuriant. The coastal stretches are marked by mangroves (where the bruguieres are predominant), ironwood trees (either casuarinas or filaos), pandanus (screw pines), sago palms and coconut trees. The equitorial type of forest has high-boled trees, including the kamerere, a giant eucalyptus which can reach up to 130 feet in height and numerous epiphyte plants. Where the natural covering has been degraded, the rain forest is replaced by thick underwoods, particularly bamboo. Between 1,650 and 3,300 feet, appear southern conifers which form the majority of wooded vegetation up to 9,800 feet on the highest islands. Evergreen oaks and beeches can also be found, as well as arborescent ferns. On the western slopes, the sparser forest takes on the appearance of grassy savanna dotted with small trees. Above 9,800 feet, the vegetation becomes scraggy and gives way to rhododendrons, then to high mountain pastures.

## A RELATIVELY POOR FLORA AND FAUNA

Apart from the large western islands, the Melanesian archipelagoes have a limited flora and fauna, even if their diversity and richness are generally superior to those of Micronesia or Polynesia. The large Melanesian islands are not far from Asiatic and Australian mainlands, and, to some extent, profit from this proximity. Most vegetable and animal species are indigenous, due to the long period of isolation of these islands for dozens of millions of years before the arrival of men who, in just a few centuries, have upset the ecosystems. Until the arrival of the Oceanians at first, then the Europeans, there were no useful

*The famous Bounty expedition set out in 1788 to find the artocarpus, or bread-fruit tree.*

plants (yams, taroes, sweet potatoes, banana trees, bread-fruit trees) and no superior mammals (dogs, pigs, rats). The flora and fauna of the smaller islands are poor in variety, even if this is often dissimulated by the luxuriance of the former and the beauty of the latter. Such lack of variety may be accounted for by the distance from the Asiatic and Australian mainlands, and becomes accentuated the further east one goes. There is no notable difference between the species of Fiji in Melanesia and those of Tonga in Polynesia.

# A PROFUSION OF PRIMITIVE MICRO-SOCIETIES

Melanesians are above all attached to the land, even if there are numerous fishing populations on the coasts. The original hunters-and-gatherers, groups of which can still be found in New Guinea, have disappeared from Melanesia. At the most, in certain of the Solomon islands or thousand individuals, whence the extreme splintering of communities. Other characteristics such as family ties or bonds of geneological consanguinity, which elsewhere in Oceania are the common rule, are less important here. What counts is the seniority of land ownership rights and the use made of them.

As in New Guinea, yam and taro competitions

Vanuatu, a few semi-nomadic clans occasionally go out hunting. And yet the Melanesians are not an authentic sedentary people, and do not hesitate to move in whole villages for the sake of a cultivating burn-baited land.

Traditional society is organized around land and its cultivation. This theoretical model has, however, given rise to a cluster of social systems, each as original as the next. In the present state of our knowledge, it is impossible to give a picture of Melanesian society in general, even if certain common characteristics are present. The first is their small size. Unlike Polynesian societies, Melanesian ones rarely exceed one confer a prestige on the winners which can promote them to the head of the clan or the village. On the other hand, anyone who does not look after his gardens is despised and can even be banned from the group.

Whether they follow consanguinity on the father's side, as in New Caledonia and the Fiji islands, or on the mother's, as in Trobriand, New Britain and the Solomon islands, or either as in Vanuatu or the western Solomons, all Melanesian societies favour landowner ground laws and ceremonial exchanges of agricultural products, certain specimens of which are regarded as highly sacred.

*The interiors of the major Melanesian islands, here that of Viti Levu, are covered by impenetrable tropical forests with dominant high-boled trees and arborescent ferns.*

*The world was totally bare. There was a vast land dotted with huge rocks and an immense stretch of water and an infinite sky which dominated everything, but they were motionless and empty. Nothing lived on the surface of the land, in the deeps or in the air. The world burned ceaselessly under the blinding light of the sun which, from the origins of time, had remained fixed in the midst of the sky. There was no night, just eternal day. There came a moment, however, when, under the effect of the intense heat, a big black rock called Qat Goro (or Iro Ul) exploded with a shattering noise. From it emerged a vui (spirit) whose name was Qat. The spirit looked around him and saw the desert expanses. Other rocks were also bursting apart, each engendering a vui. These primordial spirits then scattered into nature where they began to wander but were unable to sleep. Qat did not follow them. He continued to contemplate the sterile world which surrounded him and found it ugly. As the firstborn of the spirits, he was the most powerful. He decided to use his powers to create living creatures who, by populating the world, would make it a better place.*

*He began by inventing plants and trees which he sowed in the ground, and algae which he hid away under the water. Then he created the animals of the earth, the air and the sea and placed them in their respective environments. But, fixed at its zenith, the burning heat of the sun, invariably dried up whatever he made. Qat had to find a way of protecting his creation. He knew that, in a far-off island, lived an old god I Qong and his daughter Qong, night. He chose a pig, taroes and yams and attached them to his dugout canoe. He took to the sea and set out for the island where I Qong lived. Once there, he offered the old god the animal and the plants in exchange for his daughter Qong. The god accepted the offer. Qat brought night back in his boat. He hid her in his house and went to speak to the sun. After long discussions and with the help of numerous presents, he managed to convince the star to divide time into equal days, then to accept that, for half of each day, Qong would cover the sky. Since this agreement, the sun and the night have alternately shared the sky. Qat completed his work by setting time in motion. From then*

*owards the seasons came round at regular intervals, the rains watered the earth, the winds rose and the tides moved the Ocean. The other vui had witnessed Qat's exploits from afar and they were envious of his power and guile. And so, when he called them to him, they came without hesitation. He taught them how to sleep each time the night came and how to create some vegetable and animal species. And yet he was still dissatisfied. Something was missing in this new world: a master, a superior being, capable of giving it order.*

*Qat therefore decided to create humanity. He chose a fine, dark-barked and smooth-trunked tree. Out of it he carved the bodies of three men and three women. Once he had carefully polished them, he set them down in the shelter of a thick clump of trees. After three days, he removed the carvings from their shelter. He lined them up in two rows, the women in front and the men behind. Firstly he invoked the forces of the earth, sky and water. Then he played his drum and life entered the effigies. Finally he danced and the carvings came to life. This was the birth of the first three human couples. As one, they thanked the vui, who was very proud of his creatures.*

*Soon afterwards, Qat began to teach them the secrets of nature. He taught them how to grow taroes, yams and sweet potatoes. He passed on the art of hunting and fishing. He showed them how to make fire and cook food. The first human beings had children who had children who, in their turn, had others. Humanity multiplied and, each day, paid tribute to its creator. All the other vui beheld the work of Qat in wonder. All except one, called Marawa, the spider spirit, who was eaten with jealousy. His power was almost the equal of that of Qat. He also wished to be worshipped by human beings. He had closely observed Qat when he created the first couples. Scrupulously imitating his rival's gestures, he carried out the carvings in a dark-barked, smooth-trunked tree and hid them in a bush. Three days later, he breathed life and movement into them by playing the drum and dancing. But when he saw them moving, he was afraid that he would not be able to control them and so buried them in a hole which he covered with leaves. One week later, overcome by remorse, he returned to remove the effigies from their pit. Alas, he had left them there too long and, when he took them out, they were*

# The legend of Qat

*All Melanesian cosmogonies affirm that the world was "set in movement" by a hero-creator of whom the following legend, from the Banks islands, is the perfect archetype.*

half decomposed. Shamed by his failure, he went to the garden that Qat's men were tending and buried the rest of his creatures there. The taroes and yams gradually absorbed the rotting matter. When the men ate their vegetables, their skin began to peel. After some time, they completely changed their skin. Then the phenomenon of shedding the skin happened at regular intervals. And the more they changed skin, the worse they became. They became jealous of each other and fought amongst themselves. Soon they began to fight and inflict serious wounds on each other. In the end, they separated into rival clans, and war broke out to take possession of land. Qat did not understand the violence of his creatures and had to resolve a serious problem. As death did not exist, the number of men ceaselessly increased, but the surface of the earth remained the same. Qat decided to appeal to Mate, death. The black Mate lived in the underworld of Panoã. He listened to the vui's sad words and accepted to come up to the surface of the earth during the night. The men were asleep. Mate introduced a part of death into each of them which would grow with time.

When it had taken possession of the whole of a human being, the latter had to descend into the land of Panoã. Humanity's destiny was sealed. But Qat did not want man alone to disappear within the creation. And so he decided that every living creature on the earth, in the Ocean and skies would undergo the same fate until the end of time. So it was that, through the stupid fault of Marawa, each living creature was henceforth condemned to grow old and die.

*A fishing village on the small island of Kaileuna.*
*Fishing is the islanders' only activity,*
*for whom it is a meagre source of subsistence.*

The term Papuan archipelagoes covers a large number of Melanesian islands, divided into two main groups, the Bismarck archipelago to the north and, to the south, the Milne Bay group and Louisiade archipelago. All these islands belong politically to Papua New Guinea, but geographically and culturally to Melanesia. From a geological point of view, however, the Bismarck archipelago, which is part of the external Melanesian belt, should be distinguished from the other archipelagoes which are part of the same structure as New Guinea.

Although governed by Papua New Guinea, the islands of Buka and Bougainville belong geologically and culturally to the Solomon archipelago.

## THE PAPUAN-MELANESIAN ETHNIC MUDDLE

The total population living in the Papuan archipelagoes does not exceed 470,000 inhabitants for 62,500 km² of landmass in the midst of a marine surface area of 1,350,000 km², excluding the islands of Buka and Bougainville. These archipelagoes are inhabited by ethnic groups of Papuan and Melanesian origin who, together, make up 98% of the population, the remaining 2% being made up by non-Melanesian Oceanians and Asians. The ethnic mix has been so intense over the centuries that, except in certain "pockets" of New Britain and New Ireland, it is impossible to tell Papuan and Melanesian apart. Certain anthropologists manage, however, to distinguish people of Papuan extract with a dolichocephalic skull from those of Melanesian origin with a monocephalic skull. But their attempt to differentiate is far from meeting with the entire approval of the scientific community which, for the moment, simply talks of an "ethnic muddle" that requires much research before yielding its secrets.

## THE NORTHERN GROUP OF THE MAJOR ISLANDS

The group of Papuan archipelagoes to the north groups the Admiralty islands (2,100 km²), the Saint Matthias islands (900 km²), the Bismarck archipelago, that is to say Lavongai, ex New Hanover (2,000 km²), New Britain (37,000 km²),

# 4
## 2

# THE PAPUAN ARCHIPELAGOES

New Ireland (9,600 km²), the Duke of York islands (57 km²), as well as many small coral islands such as Tabar, Lihir, Tanga and Feni. The geological history of this zone is linked to that of the external Melanesian belt. The oldest rocks (from the Paleozoic to the Mesozoic period) are present in the centre of new Britain. Tertiary sedimentary formations (from Eocene to Pliocene periods) as well as quaternary volcanic rocks are present everywhere. Late uplift movements gave most of the archipelago islands an asymmetrical appearance. To the north-west, the Admiralty islands are made up of a large volcanic island, called Manus, and several small coral islands. The Saint Matthias group has a similar morphology to that of New Ireland. The Duke of York goup is made up of thirteen small coral islands separating New Britain from New Ireland, two very large islands with the most marked geological features. The former, essentially made up of tertiary volcanic rocks, often covered with coral sediments, undergoes strong volcanic activity and is associated with significant subsidence phenomena. There is no volcanic activity on the second, however, where eruptive rocks (basalts, trachytes, andesites) are covered by thick layers of Pliocene sandstone and limestone. The islands have a mountain relief. Many summits are over 6,500 feet in height in New Britain, where Mount Sinewit reaches 7,996 feet.

Many of the northern group of islands undergo intense seismic and volcanic activity (volcanoes, geysers, sulphur springs, smoke holes) above fault lines resulting from the shearing of the oceanic plate.

These archipelagoes were discovered in the 17th Century. In 1616, the Dutch Schouten and Lemaire visited Manus island (future Admiralty islands). In 1690 the Englishman Dampier gave the name Nova Britannia to the large southern island. In 1767, another Englishman, Carteret, gave names to New Ireland, New Hanover and Admirality. All the Papuan archipelagoes were visited by Europeans for over a century without anyone really settling there. When the English, however, and the Germans from 1885, undertook colonization for economic and military ends,

In most of the Papuan archipelagoes,
here the Lihir islands, the arrival
of shoals of fish is the occasion
for joyous bouts of collective fishing.
By striking the water hard, young
boys drive the fish out to the open sea
where the men are waiting for them
with their nets.

Community spirit
is strong everywhere.
Whether it be in the building
of large ceremonial boats
or everyday fishing,
all villagers take an active part.

violent clashes occurred with the natives. In the midst of diseases, massacres and deportations which decimated the local population, New Ireland became New Mecklenbourg and New Britain New Pomerania, to regain their original names at the end of World War I, after the German defeat. Placed under Australian trustee-ship in 1921 by the League of Nations, these islands enjoyed a relative peace which enabled the populations to be reconstituted thanks to a high birth rate. Today 372,000 people live in this region, of which 256,000 in New Britain, 82,000 in New Ireland and 31,000 on the Admiralty islands.

## THE ARCHIPELAGOES OF THE SOUTHERN GROUP

The southern Papuan archipelagoes are much smaller and more fragmented than their northern counterparts. They group together a host of islands and reefs, of volcanic or coral origin, situated in the Solomon Sea. The province of Milne Bay includes the Trobriand islands, or Kiriwina (440 km²), Woodlark island or Murua (900 km²), the Entrecasteaux islands (3,800 km²) including Goodenough, Fergusson and Normanby, the Louisiade archipelago (2,200 km²) with a dozen or so islands including Misima, Tagula and Yela and a myriad of reefs. Together with their numerous dependencies, these islands are situated on the shallow continental shelf surrounding New Guinea. This shelf, on which the last mountainous advances of the Huon peninsula rest, lies between the Solomon and the Coral Seas, becoming more and more fragmented as it goes. The result is a double insular morpho-logy with average-sized volcanic islands and small coral-reef islands. The former, represented by the Entrecasteaux group, near to the east coast of New Guinea, are the continuation, in a south-easterly direction, of the Owen Stanley Range. The relief of these islands is of a massive and jagged nature with several peaks over 6,500 feet in height and situated in a zone marked by strong volcanic activity. Their geomorphology is identical to the mountains of which they are an extension, with abundant metamorphic forma-tions and the presence of effusive eruptive rocks. The islands of Trobriand, Woodlark and the Louisiade archipelago, on the other hand, are flat, low coral islands.

Doubtless on account of the their lack of economic and strategic interest, all these islands were discovered relatively late by Europeans, from Vaez de Torres in 1606 to La Perouse in

*In the Papuan archipelagoes, rowing is a means of covering short distances or performing ritual journeys, such as the "kula". Sails, more often than not woven from pandanus or screw pine leaves, enable longer trips to be made.*

117

*The big chief of Omakarana on the island of Kiriwina*
*is traditionally the most important figure in the Trobriand archipelago.*
*The size of his large yam graneries attests his social standing.*

1787, and inbetweentime Entrecasteaux and Trobriand.

Contrary to the general rule, their relative isolation from the rest of the external world enabled them to escape violent colonization.

Late arrivals also, the missionaries spared native traditions all the more so. Although European diseases created victims, there was no incidence of massacres nor massive deportations. The population, which today numbers 85,000, has undergone no, or relatively little mixing. It has remained more or less pure and is extremely attached to its traditions, the most exceptional

being that of the kula, a complex network of ceremonial exchanges (shell money and mother-of-pearl bracelets) which take place within a circular marine zone encompassing all the southern archipelagoes. This ancient ritual, performed using large decorated canoes, originally enabled the limitation of confrontations between islands which were united by the magical bond of exchange.

*Yam growing is the basis of food in the area,*
*but also a social basis in the "kula" islands*
*(Trobriand, Iwa, Woodlark, Misima, Panaete, Wari, Entrecasteaux, Amphlett...).*
*A veritable cult is devoted to tubers, culminating at harvest time.*
*In accordance with tradition, it is the wife's brother*
*who fills his brother-in-law's granery who returns the compliment*
*to his sisters' husbands.*

*Several of the Papuan archipelago societies are of a matriarchal type.*
*It is the women who carve the totemic figures that protect the tribe.*

◄

*A woman from the Woodlark islands displays mother-of-pearl,*
*indicating her social status, whilst the Goodenough islander,*
*as most Melanesians, chews his daily betel.*

►

*A rare ceremony for the inhabitants of Kiriwina.*
*The men from a Tabalu clan, who provide the most important chiefs in the Trobriand islands,*
*take symbolic possession of the village "deserted" by the women at the end of the yam harvest.*

*Far from the madding trade routes,*
*the rhythm of life seems unchanging*
*in this small Lavongai village.*

*Women in the western islands,*
*particularly in the Entrecasteaux*
*archipelago, commonly tatoo their faces.*

◄

*The pandanus or screw pine is a providential tree for islanders.*
*Trunk and roots are used as construction material or firewood,*
*whilst the leaves are used to make sails.*

*Situated mid-way between Guadalcanal and Malaita,*
*the two largest of the Solomon islands,*
*the Nggela islands are here silhouetted against the golden evening sun.*

The Solomon and Vanuatu islands present a remarkable geographical and human continuity. They are two impressive, undersea volcanic arcs topped by tall islands, that follow in succession. Their populations are unquestionably linked from an ethnic and cultural point of view, which is the reason we have chosen to study them together in this chapter.

## THE SOLOMON AND VANUATU ISLANDS: TWIN ARCHIPELAGOES

Independent since 1978, the State of the Solomon islands is part of the British Commonwealth. Vanuatu (ex New Hebrides), which was a territory under Anglo-French condiminium, became an independent republic in 1980. The Solomon islands have a surface area of 28,500 km² for a marine surface area of 1,340,000 km². The two main groups of islands are the Solomons themselves, two of which, Buka and Bougainville, are governed by Papua New Guinea, and the Santa Cruz group, several hundred kilometres to the east with much smaller islands. In addition, there are other islands and archipelagoes situated still further east (Duff, Tikopia, Fataka, Cherry), atolls (Ontong, Java, Rennell, Sikaiana, Bellona), and a large number of uninhabited islands and reefs. The Solomon archipelago itself is made up of six main islands, Choiseul (or Lauru), Santa Isabel, Malaita, San Cristobal, New Georgia and Guadalcanal where the capital, Honiara, is situated, together with twenty or so medium-sized islands and numerous small ones.

From Buka and Bougainville (which geographically belongs to it) to the Santa Cruz islands, the archipelago forms part of the external Melanesian belt and includes the highest parts of the long underwater range stretching from the Bismarck archipelago to Vanuatu in a north-west to south-east arc. The main group is spaced out along two almost parallel axes which suddenly converge at each of their extremities. Situated along the external or frontal alignement, Choiseul, Santa Isabel and Malaita have a narrow and elongated shape due to the narrowness of the underwater mountain base on which they are situated.

# 4 / 3

# SOLOMON & VANUATU

Bougainville, New Georgia, San Cristobal, on the other hand, which are situated on a more extensive base, are wider. Almost all of these islands have a rough mountainous aspect, as a result of an omnipresent volcanic activity, either active as in Bougainville (Bagana and Takuan volcanoes) or underlying, as in most of the other islands. Even the atolls which are situated on volcanic reliefs that have disappeared, are subject to such activity.

Throughout the high islands, the rock formations, where the substratum which generally dates from the Cretaceous-Eocene period (andesites, basalts) has been covered by ultrabasic rocks and deposits that have been violently folded then broken, are marked by innumerable orogenic movements. Parts that have emerged, then been eroded, have been raised once more above sea-level, whilst others have broken up and sunk forever. Sandy atolls (Ontong Java) or raised ones (Rennell), formed by coral, are situated on a volcanic substratum (schists) which has gradually slipped down into the ocean.

Vanuatu is made up of thirteen large islands, thirty or so small ones and numerous reefs which stretch along two axes, in a north-west to south-east direction, either side of a line of partly underwater, active volcanoes, and which come together in their southern extremity. The total landmass is 12,200 km² spread over a marine surface area of 680,000 km². Six out of the thirteen major islands are situated in an inner arc: Espiritu Santo (or Santo), Malekula (or Mallicolo), Vate (or Efate) with the capital town of Port Vila, Eromanga (or Erromango), Tanna and Aneityum (or Anatom). The other seven, Vanua, Lava, Gaua (or Sainte Marie), Oba (or Aoba), Maewo (or Aurora), Pentecost (or Raga), Ambrym and Epi are aligned along an external (or frontal) arc. These mountainous, volcanic islands are each hinged by massive rock formations, on the sides of which large valleys open up. A narrow coastal strip stretches along the foot of the mountain mass. The coasts are surrounded by abundant reef formations. The whole archipelago is characterized by volcanic activity, in particular at the meeting place of the two structural arcs (the

*In the Kwara'ae ethnic group,*
*certain fair-haired boys are considered*
*as being the descendants of the large white shark,*
*founder of the first clans.*
*With their friends, they take part in the making of "tafuliae",*
*the old sea-shell money.*
*Once the shells have been polished by the children,*
*they are baked and take on a different colour which defines their value.*

Shepherd islands, Epi, Lopevi) which is a zone of continual and violent telluric phenomena that has even undergone veritable volcano-tectonic cataclysms, in particular those that occurred in 1350 and 1700 of sad memory.

Vanuatu is the extension of the immense arc of underwater mountains linking it to the Bismarck archipelago, taking in that of the Solomon islands. The line of volcanoes which gave rise to Vanuatu doubtless began to be formed in the ocean depths from the Pliocene period onwards on crystalline substratum (diorites, quartz,

Benbow (on Ambrym island), Iahue (on Tanna) and Lopevi, in the open sea, which comes to life from time to time.

## FEARSOME TRIBES

The populations of the Solomon and Vanuatu archipelagoes are 342,000 and 157,000 inhabitants respectively. 96% are Melanesians with Micronesians, Polynesians, Europeans and Asians making up the remaining 4%. For a long time adventurers and missionaries gave these islands a wide berth on account of their reputation. The

granites). The external arc, which is like an impressive fault-ridden horst, was lifted up at the time and continues to be so. The geological history of the internal arc is somewhat different. During the Oligocene period, thick layers of sediments (tuffs, marl, limestone) were deposited up to the Miocene period and andesic eruptions began once more in the Pliocene. From then on, the two arcs were ceaselessly raised by stages, brought on by periods of statis. Dislocated by numerous faults, the substratum gave way to volcanoes, some of which remained below the sea whilst others emerged.

There are only three volcanoes active today,

capitals of Europe echoed with the most terrifying tales of fierce headhunters or cannibals that peopled these mysterious lands covered with impenetrable vegetation. The warlike violence of the natives was no legend and inter-tribal or inter-island confrontations were a permanent feature of life. Even today, the Kwaio of Malaita or the Mbotgote of Malekula strike fear into their neighbours.

*The coastal villages of the Solomon archipelago, here Lilisiana, look alike. Houses on piles are built near to the beach. Daily activity is centered exclusively around the ocean.*

## THE BRUTAL CLASH OF COLONIZATION

Although there are no precise figures for the populations of these two archipelagoes prior to the arrival of the Europeans, approximately 600,000 people are estimated to have been living in the Solomons and a little under 400,000 in Vanuatu. In 1568, Hernando Gallego, a member of the Mendaña expedition, landed on the Solomon islands and in 1606, Vanuatu was discovered by the Portuguese explorer Fernandes de Queiros, only to be forgotten by the world for over one and a half centuries. Often badly noted on sea charts, these islands seemed to be of no interest at all, either economic or strategic, to European powers. It was not until 1768 that the

Frenchman Bougainville rediscovered them and brought them to international attention. The result was not long in coming. Solomon and Vanuatu, called successively Australia del Spiritu Santo by the Portuguese, then Grandes Cyclades by the French and finally New Hebrides by the British, were the sites of violent occupation. Missionaries carried out forced conversions whilst settlers, with the support of the army, hunted down the Melanesian tribes. Diseases brought in from Europe decimated the villages.

Entire ethnic groups were deported to serve as labour in Australian plantations or in other Pacific colonies. The islanders of the Solomons showed such aggressive resistance that the Europeans hesitated penetrating into the interior and left the natives to live in the shelter of the mountains and forests. Vanuatu, however, despite the desperate resistance of certain tribes, bore the full lash of the colonial machine. At the end of the 19th Century, the Melanesian population of the Solomons had been reduced to 100,000 and that

*More than elsewhere in Melanesia, children are treated in a privileged manner. Collective celebrations are regularly organized in their honour.*

*In numerous islands, the "kastom" requires that the skulls of the "great ancestors", that is to say the dead sorcerer-priests, be kept in sacred enclosures.*

*In the traditional villages of the Solomon islands,*
*raised houses are reserved for young males*
*during their period of initiation.*

*A façade of palm leaves,*
*dyed and woven, characteristic*
*of the Makira province.*

*The coasts of New Georgia and Choiseul
are indented by many small coves,
giving shelter to a fishing population that lives in isolation.*

of the Vanuatu to less than 70,000. It was only after the Second World War that the demographic tendency was reversed, with a strong annual increase around 3.3% for the Solomons and 2.5% for the Vanuatu, a tendency which has been further accentuated by independence, to the point where, today, the authorities are wondering if the islands can be self-sufficient. For the moment, there are enough food crops (tubers, rice) to feed the population, but for how long? The coconut trade and its derivates (copra in particular) still constitute one quarter of agricultural activity, despite a fall-off in demand, and fishing is a source of income not to be neglected. In the poorer Vanuatu, cocoa and coffee plantations, as well as livestock, all brought in by European settlers, represent over half the country's resources.

## KASTOM

*Kastom* is the pidgin term for "custom". It covers all customs and rituals which form the very basis of the Melanesian society of the Solomons and Vanuatu. Traditional life in the villages, where 80% of the population live, is governed by ancient rules which are deemed to be good and unquestionable because they were used by ancestors who have today disappeared but who continue to protect the clans. Since the relationship between the world of the living and that of the dead is permanent, kastom is impregnated with magic. The spirit of those who have disappeared can therefore be reincarnated in animals or trees and be invoked according to certain precise rites known only to the initiated and the sorcerers. Belief in ghosts, ogres, evil spells, similar to those in New Guinea, here reach a culminating point. The social group is therefore dominated by two categories of men, the sorcerer who possesses the secrets of the invisible world and the big man who is the emanation of the council of family chiefs. At the heart of these warfaring societies, the feeling of belonging to a clan is very strong. All its members are wantok (pidgin for one talk), that is to say they speak the same language, which is a vivid way of affirming their indestructible mutual support. This conception sometimes implicates whole villages to take up the cause of the dispute, even if it is ill-founded, of one of their own and to fight with neighbouring tribes.

*In the interior of the large mountainous islands,*
*populations refuse contact with the modern world.*
*War is a living reality.*
*Certain ethnic groups are known and feared*
*throughout the archipelago,*
*such as the Kwaio from Malaita,*
*to whom this proud warrior,*
*armed with a club, belongs.*

*In the Solomons, as in Vanuatu, men often hunt in pairs,*
*for reasons of efficiency but also for safety in case of an unforeseen encounter.*

*Forest forays, in pursuit of rare game, are long.*
*The hunters spend many days away from their homes*
*and must adapt themselves to a hostile environment,*
*like this inhabitant of Bunlap, on the island of Pentecost,*
*who is preparing to sleep in a makeshift cabin.*

*Like many of his compatriots,
this fisherman from Malekula,
is used to waiting, motionless and silent,
for the fish to come close to his small nets.*

*The effects of typhoons are felt
well beyond their zones of activity.
This is Erromango in Vanuatu in 1992,
after the Val cyclone had affected
the Samoan islands in the same year,
some 2,000 kms away!*

*The western coast of la Grande Terre between Hiengbene and Pouebo
is bordered by the high mountain mass of Panié,
covered by a tropical forest, from where numerous waterfalls run down.*

The French overseas Territory of New Caledonia, whose capital is NoumEa, occupies a marine surface area of 1,740,000 km², of which 19,160 km² is emerged land. It includes la Grande Terre, l'åle des Pins, the Loyalty islands (Ouvéa, Lifou, Maré), several archipelagoes (the Chesterfield islands, Bélep, Huon, Surprise, Walpole) and numerous uninhabited reefs.

## A COMPLETE GEOLOGICAL STRUCTURE

The main island is one of the largest in Melanesia, whence the name Grande Terre or Great Land. It is a mountainous island with a massive, continental structure. The impressive mountainous complex which provides a framework to the island along its whole length, becomes gradually lower towards the south-east. To the north-west, it is divided into two high, parallel ranges encompassing the wide Diahot valley. Mount Panié culminates in the eastern range at 5,340 feet. The coastal plains are relatively narrow to the west and almost inexistant to the east. Off-shore, there is an impressive coral barrier reef which surrounds the island for over 1,600 km. At the south-east of Grande Terre rises the åle des Pins, whose name comes from the monkey-puzzle trees which cover it. The Loyalty islands are situated some 150 kms from Grande Terre, on a volcanic line which runs parallel to it. Although they are of the same geological type as Grande Terre, they do not have its mountainous aspect. They are in the form of atolls, raised in Lifou and Maré, whereas in Ouvéa, the largest part of the atoll, the sloped formation finally disappears into the lagoon. Their asymmetrical morphology results from the fact that, during the Pleistocene period, the archipelago was tilted towards the north-west. All other atolls are low and flat islands around a central lagoon.

From a geological point of view, the Grande Terre is a paradise for specialists. Two major items make this island a unique case in the Pacific: with the exception of the Lower and Middle Cretaceous periods, all types of rock strata are represented from the Permian to the present day, including in particular the widest

# 4/4
# NEW CALEDONIA

expanse of ultrabasite outcrops in the world which, after weathering, have given exceptional nickel deposits providing the mainstream of the island's economy. The clear-cut nature of the different layers gives affords an excellent geological history of the region. During a first phase which lasted from the Permian to the Jurassic, sediments were deposited. After a volcanic period (during the Jurassic), a substantial orogenic phase produced an initial underwater mountainous arc. Alternance between sedimentation and volcanic phases, followed by a long period of complex movements (fault fractures and slips, compressions, chipping) occurred during the Middle Eocene period. In the Oligocene, a second mountainous arc appeared to the north. The Miocene brought detrital deposits. Afterwards, and up to the end of the Plio-Quaternary, various compressive or fracturing tectonic phases shaped the relief. The coral reefs then began to form.

## NIAOULI AND CAGOU

New Caledonia is a naturalist's paradise, with a wide variety of species, 80% of which are indigenous. Over 2,000 rare plants have been indexed, amongst which the monkey-puzzle trees or Cook's araucaria, the bouaro whose leaves are chewed by the Kanaks, the *koku* whose fine wood is used for timber frames, the *dis* (or *dja*) used for thatching the native huts, *heteropogon* (or *andropogan*), a prickle grass, gaic, an acacia whose appearance recalls the olive tree, the giant *kauri* (which can grow up to 160 feet in height) and above all the niaouli which has become the emblem-tree of New Caledonia. To give it its scientific name, the niaouli, *Melaleuca leucadron* or *Melaleuca viridiflora*, is widespread in the Caledonian forests above 1,650 feet. It belongs to the Myrtaceae family, like the eucalyptus. Dear to the heart of the native inhabitants, it is reputed to clean the air and has medicinal virtues. It was from the distillation of its leaves in 1880 that petroleum jelly or soothing oil was extracted (goménol in French from the name of the Gomen tribe) used for rhinopharyngeal treatments. Another particularity is that it does not burn during forest fires, from which it exits black but unscathed.

*A superb specimen of thunbergia brought from India by man and which has become perfectly adapted to Grande Terre.*

*The land situated to the west of the central range belongs to the Caldoches, or white New Caledonians. It is an area of niaouli savanna where extensive livestock rearing is everywhere present.*

*The niaouli, the sweet-smelling, emblematic tree of New-Caledonia, has a tough bark which protects it from fires.*

Animal life offers a dual aspect. Although fauna of the land and air is poor, its marine counterpart compensates by its richness. There are practically no mammals, except for the flying fox and those brought in by man, and reptiles are uncommon. Insects and birds are few in number. There are less than 100 varieties of birds indexed, of which only 18 are indigenous. The most well-known are the *notou*, a large white pigeon which, together with the flying fox, formerly constituted the only game of the Kanaks, and the *cagou* which has, like the *niaouli*, become a symbol of the country. The *cagou* or *Rhinochaetus jubatus*, is unique. It is the size of a hen, has a grey-blue plumage with white and black wing quills and a crest which it makes bristle when it is angry. Its cry ressembles the barking of a dog. It is a running-bird which has lost the use of its wings, just like the New Zealand *kiwi*.

## THE KANAKS

The Kanaks have certain racial characteristics which make them akin to the Australian Aborigines. Today there are 78,000 of them, about 44% of the total population of New Caledonia. The other inhabitants are white and of European stock, mainly French, representing 36% of the population, Polynesian (14%) and Asians (6%).

MELANESIANS DISPOSSESSED OF THEIR LAND

At the beginning of colonization, after Captain Cook had discovered Grande Terre in 1774, which he called New Caledonia, the Kanaks, who had for a long time remained isolated from the rest of the world, numbered 50,000.

Missionaries, adventurers and traffickers came in the wake of navigators. Amongst these were whale hunters, sandalwood traders (Grande Terre was particularly rich in this variety of tree), and beachcombers (fishers of holothurians [sea cucumbers] which were much sought after by Chinese pharmacopoeia) all of whom carried out their activities from the 19th Century onwards. Clashes with local populations multiplied and degenerated into a wave of murderous conflicts. In 1853, Napoleon III decided to annex it to set up a prison there and in 1860, it officially became a French colony. Sailors and colonialists, especially livestock breeders, settled in mass, systematically dispossessing the Kanaks of their lands and killing those who resisted.

Expropriations and murders reached such a scale that conflicts, which up to then had remained isolated, turned into a general uprising which set

A Kanak from the Bondé tribe
crossing the Diahot swollen by rain
on a home-made raft.

One of the numerous varieties
of bauhinia on the island.

The cagou is a running-bird
native to New Caledonia.
There are estimated
to be less than 2,000 specimens.

*The traditional Kanak hut has a rounded shape.*
*Its walls are made from "niaouli skins" (bark) according to the local expression.*
*The roof is topped by a ridge spire which has protective virtues.*

the country ablaze from 1878 to 1880. Repression was bloody. At the end of the 19th Century, the discovery of gold and copper mines, followed by exceptional deposits of nickel (which even today places New Caledonia as the world's third largest producer) gave rise to a second rush of immigrants. The Kanaks were again driven from their lands and many were killed. At the outset of the 20th Century, their number had been reduced by half. After the Second World War, the birth rate of the Melanesian population underwent a rapid increase, some 1.5% per year. Political problems between Kanaks, many of whom want their independence, and France remain. The tragic events of 1988 remind us of the wall of incomprehension, sometimes hatred, which exists between the two communities. The Caldoches (New Caledonians of European stock), living for the most part on the west coast, are encamped on their large properties facing the Kanaks who are concentrated in the central mountains and the east coast of Grande Terre as well as on the surrounding islands.

## TRIBES AND CHIEFTAINRY

Kanak social organization is the most elaborate in Melanesia. It is based on the tribe, a patch of land left to the natives by the colonising process and which the whole clan owns in common.

Everything that exists and lives on this territory is part of the tribe and subject to customary law. Its management is ensured by a chieftainry system by which the councils of the senior members delegate their power to "little chiefs", who in turn report to a "big chief" who incarnates the relation between deceased ancestors and the world of the living. This confers the right to own a "Big hut", which is the Caledonian equivalent of the New Guinean "Men's hut". The ritual objects such as flutes, drums and sacred effigies which enable him to communicate with the dead are kept here under his protection. It is generally the "little chiefs" who ensure liaison between the French authorities and the tribe, whereas the "big chief" is in charge of the customary running of the community.

New Caledonia has neither the vigour
nor the genius of Melanesian carving.
Nevertheless, some artists, such as this carver
from the Gohapin tribe, manage to create
an original art that draws its source from tradition.

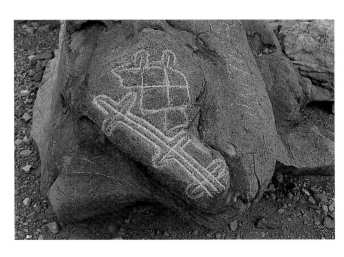

◀◀◀

Grande Terre has surprising petroglyphs
which have not yet yielded up all their secrets.
Some specialists think that they are the result
of a mysterious culture which reached its zenith
between the second millenium and 500 BC.

*Society is subjected to strict patrilocal customs.*
*When the master of the house dies, everything goes as of right*
*to the male members of the husband's clan.*


*The horse was introduced by Europeans in the 18ᵗʰ Century,*
*much to the fright of the Kanaks of the period.*
*Their present-day descendants have, however,*
*adopted it as a privileged form of transport in the mountains.*

*Teachers from Nouville
wearing the famous "missionary-dress"
take time off during recreation.*

*The island of Mbengga
and its dependencies seen from the southern coast of Viti Levu.*

# 4/5

# FIJI

The republic of Fiji, which left the British Commonwealth in 1988, following serious ethnic conflicts, to become fully independent, is situated at the junction between Melanesia and Polynesia. Its land surface area is 18,280 km² for a sea area of 1,290,000 km². The Fiji islands are disposed in a vast arc of a circle open to the south. They include the two major islands of Viti Levu (10,500 km²) with Suva, the capital, and Vanua Levu (5,540 km²), five medium-sized islands (Taveuni, Koro, Ngau, Ovalau, Kandavu), and three hundred small islands, only one third of which are inhabited, spread for the most part in the Yasawa archipelagoes (or western group) and those of the Koro sea, in particular the Lomaiviti archipelago (or central group) and that of Lau (or eastern group). In addition there is a multitude of small islands and reefs.

## HUGE MOUNTAIN FORMATIONS

Generally surrounded by barrier reefs, the main islands are made up of relatively high mountainous blocks. Mean altitude is about 3,300 feet in the interior. The compact mountainous mass is cut by deep valleys, along which silt has been carried to the coasts where small sedimentary plains have been built up. The medium-sized islands of the central group have a similar morphology. Maximum relief height, however, never exceeds 2,000 feet. As for the small islands, these for the main part are atolls which hardly rise above sea level.

Fiji is situated on the same continental shelf as the Tonga islands. This shelf, to the west of the deep Trenches of Tonga (-34,876 feet) and Kermadec (-31,081 feet), and of which the island of Rotuma occupies the northern extremity, is interrupted in the west at the Yasawa Trench (-16,278 feet). Although the Fiji islands have an essentially volcanic origin, they belong structurally to the external Melanesian belt. The strata common to this zone can be found in the form of a substratum where the tertiary formations of the deep level, intersected by granite and gabbroic intrusions, are covered by an extremely deformed complex of volcanic rocks (andesites,

basalts) from the Miocene to Pliocene periods. As in the other archipelagoes of the external Melanesian belt, coastal morphology and the abundance of limestone deposits bear witness to numerous phases of emergence and immersion to which the blocks of the continental shelf have been subjected.

## MELANESIANS APART

The Fiji archipelagoes were discovered in 1643 by the Dutchman Tasman, then, like many other Oceanian lands, forgotten by Europe. From the end of the 18th Century to the end of the 19th, the English first of all, then the Russians, the French, followed by the Americans, explored them. The islands were rich in sandalwood and the fertile land enabled sugar cane to be planted. After losing their battle against the Whites, the Fijians were subjected to one of the most pitiless slave trades that the Pacific has known. Not until 1874, when the islands became a British colony, were their fundamental rights recognized. After an often stormy period of cooperation, Fiji became an independent state in 1970 within the British Commonwealth, which they were forced to leave some twenty years later.

The first discoverers had noted the Fijians' racial peculiarities, with an obvious Polynesian mix. The Fiji islands are a buffer zone, from both historical and ethnic points of view, between Melanesia and Polynesia.

### THE MELANESIAN-POLYNESIAN PEOPLE

From the original peopling of the islands at around the beginning of the Christian era, the two ethnic components have constantly been mixed. The first Polynesian inhabitants were driven out by the incoming Melanesians, but numerous groups remained and became assimilated with the latter. Later, during frequent warfaring expeditions or regular exchanges of trade, the Polynesian and Melanesian populations were intermixed. The Melanesians, who have made up the majority of Fijians since the second century BC, have racially and culturally dominated the country. Polynesian incursions have, however,

never ceased during the course of the centuries, particularly in the eastern islands. The majority of islanders on Lau are today of Polynesian stock. Whether it be in the genetic or cultural field, certain recurrent Polynesian traits are clearly present within the Melanesian populations of Fiji. In general terms, their flesh-tint is lighter than that of other Melanesian peoples and their tall stature and solid bone framework are reminiscent of that of the Polynesians. Their elaborate myths are based on a logical and complex structure which is not to be found with other Melanesians but is present in Polynesia and Micronesia. Finally, the relatively elaborate structure of the social systems place them mid-way between Melanesia and Polynesia.

## A THREATENED MELANESIAN IDENTITY

Today the Fijians number 740,000. But the Melanesians who represented the majority of inhabitants (90%) at the time of colonization by the Europeans in the 18th Century, today represent less than half the population, 46% exactly. As elsewhere, the combined effects of diseases brought from Europe, exaggerated evangelization and colonial extortions drastically reduced the number of natives. At the beginning of the 20th Century, and in the wake of the terrible flu epidemic of 1919, there remained a mere 87,000, as against, according to estimations, some 200,000 when the Whites arrived. But, whereas in other Oceanian archipelagoes the arrival of the modern world enabled the native birth rate to take off again, Fiji underwent a massive wave of new immigration instigated by the colonial powers. The immigrants were Indian who came to supplement insufficient local labour for the major sugar cane plantations in particular. This migratory flow has not eased up since. From 60,000 at the beginning of the century, Indians today number 360,000, or practically half the population, the remaining 5% being made up essentially of small Oceanic and Asiatic minorities. Indians are hard-working, entrepreneurial people with a deeply imperialist mentality. Established in the coastal and trading zones, they gradually took over the economic levers of the country and created a society, with a Hindu and Muslim base, which has had a phagocytic effect on its Melanesian counterpart. Less active, the Melanesians have had to withdraw into the interior. Following the 1987 elections which installed a government dominated by the Indians, the Melanesians took up arms and attacked the Indian community. The result was a civil war which ended in 1988, but which isolated Fiji in the international field and forced them to leave the Commonwealth. Diplomatic relations with India were even cut off in 1990. Although a precarious calm reigns over the archipelago today, the Fijian Melanesians know that they will inevitably have to face up to the Indian advance or become absorbed into it

*The waters of Fiji are rich in fish,*
*with abundant pudding-wife,*
*salmon-trout and lobsters.*

◄

*Catamarans from the archipelago of Lau*
*are reputed for their reliability.*
*Recognizable by their reddish hulls and their sails*
*in woven fibres, they have been sailing*
*between the islands for over one thousand years.*

*Fishermen from Lakemba prepare to take to the open sea*
*where they will stay for several days, until their catch is sufficient.*

The interior of Vitu Levu is occupied by the high plateau of Nandrau surrounded by eroded mountains over 3,300 feet in height.

*Village women from Mbutha, in Vanua Levu, weave wall panels.*

*The village of Navala, in the central mountains of Viti Levu*
*is the largest Fijian village in the interior.*
*Its inhabitants are putting the final touch to the big hut of its customary chief.*

The rivers of the major islands
provide a much-appreciated white fish.
Collective fishing using large nets
mobilizes the whole of the village community.

*Warfaring tradition is deep-set in the Fijian soul and goes back to the time
when their expeditions spread terror throughout the surrounding archipelagoes.
Ritual celebrations are an opportunity
to recall the brave deeds of ancestors and exalt a virile force.*

*Traditional clothes are made out of "tapa", a material obtained from tree bark.*
*Whether private or public, each ceremony begins with the preparation, then the drinking of "kawa",*
*a fermented and vaguely anaesthetic drink, derived from the roots of the wild pepper plant.*

*Walking on a bed of white-hot stones is a speciality of the Mbengga islanders.*
*Certain take place on the southern coast of Viti Levu,*
*here in Pacific Harbour.*

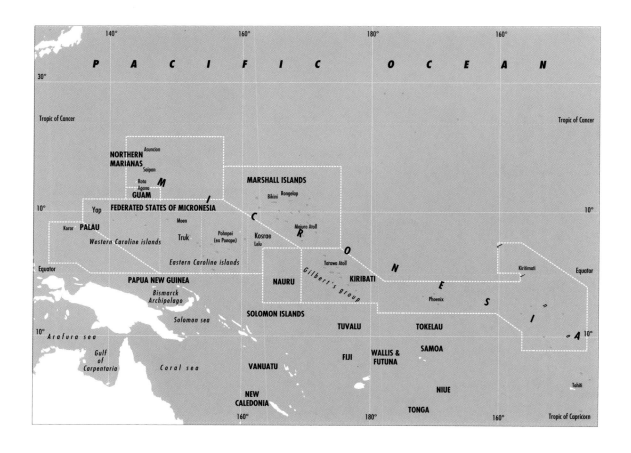

# 5
## 1

# MICRONESIA

Micronesia, which means "little islands" (from the Greek *micros* "small" and *nesos* "island") derives its name from the small size of its archipelagoes, situated in the western Pacific, north of the Equator. There are seven political entities. Two are totally independent nations: Kiribati (ex Gilbert islands) which obtained its independence from the United Kingdom in 1979, and Nauru which was granted independence from Australia in 1968. Four states have drawn up a free association agreement with the United States who granted them autonomy: the Commonwealth of the Northern Mariana islands, since 1978, the republic of the Marshall islands and the Federated States of Micronesia (ex Caroline islands) which have grouped together the insular dependencies of Yap, Truk, Pohnpei, Kosrae, since 1986, and the republic of Palau which is a special case. Although officially autonomous and associated since 1994 with the United States, it remains, as a result of a political blockage, the last American trust territory in the Pacific granted in 1947 by the U.N. Finally, Guam is a non-incorporated Territory of the United States.

## MINUTE ISLANDS WITH A TROPICAL CLIMATE

Micronesia is part of the true Pacific. Its depths are strewn with a significant network of long, underwater ranges, whose emerged summits have produced the cluster of Melanesian islands. Only a few of them have emerged as isolated relief, such as Banaba or Nauru. Geological formations are identical throughout the region. Volcanic rocks with a basalt appearance from the Tertiary and above all the Quaternary are constantly grouped with coral formations, the oldest of which date back to the Eocene period. Depending on their age and the intensity of erosion which they have undergone, the Micronesian islands have a dual aspect, often co-existing side by side. The young formations are mountainous masses, more or less jagged in appearance. The old ones take on the form of vast tables or coral atolls.

Situated in an equitorial and tropical zone, Micronesia has a warm and humid climate whose characteristics are accentuated in July-August but which attenuate the further east one goes. As a result of intertropical convergence north of the Equator, atmospheric currents push masses of air from the Tropic of Cancer to the south, which are then deviated in a north-easterly to south-westerly direction. This gives rise to the trade winds in the northern hemisphere from November to April. Temperatures rarely fall below 26°C, except in the mountains where the nights can be cool when there is rain. The annual temperature range is very narrow. Relative humidity is high to the west and moderate to the east, reaching 80% and 40% respectively. Mean annual rainfall varies in the same proportions from 4,000 to 1,800 mm of water. During winter, violent typhoons, that form on the perimeter of the Marshall and Caroline islands, occur regularly and wreak considerable damage.

## POOR FLORA AND FAUNA

As in all true Oceania, there is a flagrantly poor variety of vegetable and animal species. Despite an overall luxurance due to the combination of heat and humidity, there is little variety in the vegetation on account of the fact that the islands have been isolated for a long time. Pandanus, ironwood and coconut trees constitute the essential species. Mangroves and a prickly bush grow next to useful plants that were introduced by the first Oceanians to arrive (yams, taroes, sweet potatoes, bananas), then by Europeans (fruit, coffee and cocoa trees). Fauna is also scarce. Apart

from a few rare indigenous species, such as a variety of bat and certain birds, almost all animals were introduced by Oceanian man (dogs, rats, pigs) and by Europeans (horses, sheep, cattle).

# A HISTORY OF BLOOD AND FURY

The populations of Micronesia have undergone a particular fate. Their remoteness from the major commercial axes and the great dispersion of their islands have enabled them to preserve the bases of old socio-cultural systems up to the present day. Even today, when travelling is no longer an obstacle to the movement of population and communication, Micronesia has been little affected by tourism. This isolation has, however, failed to protect it from the violent effects of colonization and war, particularly during the 20th Century. Micronesian archipelagoes entered history as they gradually became discovered by Europeans from the 16th Century onwards. Inhabited from at least 1,700 BC, these islands, especially those to the west, already had elaborate cultures, doubtless due to repeated contacts with Asia. Thus on the Mariana islands, wheat was grown, a situation unique in Oceania, before the arrival of the Europeans. Yap reigned over a vast military and commercial empire that stretched from Palau to Truk. Noticed between 1521 and 1527 by the first Iberian navigators (Magellan, Diego da Rocha, Diego de Saavedra), most of the western Micronesian archipelagoes, with the exception of Pohnpei and Kosrae, were annexed half a century later by the Spanish crown, whilst those to the east remained relatively unknown. As always, in its wake, there swarmed the cortege of soldiers, missionaries and colonialists. The conquerors named the western islands Palaos, or Mariana and Caroline in honour of the Spanish sovereigns Marie-Anne of Habsburg, widow of Philip II and regent to the throne and Charles II. The natives attempted to resist the invasion of their lands by fierce conflict but were unable to do so for any length of time. Defeat was followed by pitiless massacre. Their number diminished tragically as the combined result of killings, disease and massive deportations to other Oceanian colonies.The entire Chamorros, Aborigines of the islands to the north of Rota in the Mariana islands, were transferred to Guam to work in the large properties of Spanish settlers.

◄ *A lone sail hastens to reach the Pagan archipelago before a violent tropical storm bursts.*

*As in most of the isolated archipelagoes of Palau, the children of Sonsorol enjoy themselves all year round in the warm water of the lagoons.*

*The small islands of the northern Mariana, here in the archipelago of Maug, are forgotten paradises where human beings are rare.*

*A variety of coral tree.*

After the missionaries had finished dismantling local socio-religious structures, other ethnic groups, imported from the Philippines and America to serve as labour in the plantations, mixed with a significant part of the original population. Although condemned by Madrid,

Spanish extortions continued up to the beginning of the 19th Century. The populations of Mariana and Yap then underwent a sharp demographic decline, losing almost half their number.

From the middle of the 18th Century, Pohnpei, Kosrae and all the eastern archipelagoes (the future Marshall islands, Nauru, Gilbert, Phoenix, Line) which had hitherto been spared, saw the arrival of other Europeans, the British in particular (Fearn, Byron, Gilbert, Marshall) and a few French.

The colonization process took place in better conditions, insofar as there were no massacres or deportations as in western Micronesia. European diseases, together with forced evangilization brought about, however, a substantial diminution in local populations. During the 19th Century, several navigators recognized the whole of Micronesia which was divided up between Spain, England and, to a lesser degree, the United States. Towards the end of the century, the expansionist appetite of another European state, Germany, became evident in the western Pacific. After annexing New Guinea and the Marshall islands in

*Island coastlines such as the one here to the south of Agrihan, are often scattered with mangroves with much half-aquatic, half-terrestrial fauna.*

1885-86, the Germans forced the Spanish to accept the arbitrage of Pope Leo XIII who, whilst recognizing Spanish sovereignty over the contested islands, also recognized commercial privileges and special property rights for the Germans which, in reality, conferred possession on them. In 1898, the United States annexed Guam, in the Mariana islands, to set up a sizeable naval base. One year later, Bismarck forced the Spanish to hand over all the other Mariana islands, as well as the Carolines and Palaos. With the outbreak of the First World War, the Japanese conquered all the Micronesian archipelagoes which remained under their control until 1945, despite American protests. Treated as second-class citizens, the fate of the Micronesians did not improve. During the Second World War, the Mariana and Caroline islands became strategic bases of prime importance for the Japanese, particularly during the South Pacific offensive of 1941-42. In 1944, the American counter-offensive drove them out after fierce fighting. Caught between cross-fire and often co-opted into a conflict which did not concern them, the natives suffered heavy losses. It is estimated that, by the end of the war, the proportion of original population, whether mixed or not, had been reduced by two-thirds in comparison to the numbers in the 16th Century! In 1947, the U.N. confided all the western Micronesian archipelagoes, as well as their eastern neighbours, to United States trusteeship. In order to replace lost labour, the latter introduced new groups, essentially from Polynesia, which gave rise to a new mix making it sometimes difficult to identify original phenotypes. Nevertheless, and for the first time since they had encountered the Whites, the rights of all Micronesians began to be respected. All the same, this does not prevent America from regarding the whole of Melanesia as private hunting ground and has led them to annex islands such as Guam or weave tight politico-economic links with freshly autonomous nations like Palau, the Northern Marianas, the Federated States of Micronesia or the Marshall islands, a number of which house American military bases.

# A SOCIETY ADAPTED
# TO A NATURAL ENVIRONMENT

Situated between Melanesia and Polynesia, and borrowing elements from each, Micronesian societies have, however, been able to invent social systems that bear an original and individual stamp, reinforced by the fact that the islands are very scattered and have sparse natural resources. Natural birth control and even the slaying of newborn babies in order to avoid overpopulation were the general rule up to the 18th or even 19th Centuries in parts. Micronesians were past masters in the art of creating and cultivating artificial gardens which they reclaimed from the lagoons. Above all, however, they set up a most elaborate social and political, mainly matrilinear society that has survived to the present day. The main feature of this society is that it is much more complex and structured from a hierarchical point of view in the high, mountainous islands, whilst being simpler and more egalitarian in the low, coral islands. It functions around the chiefs who derive their authority from their ancestry, their age, their order of birth and the size of their landed property. All the different systems, from the most complex to the simplest, are organized from this basic cell. Thus in the southern islands of Gilbert and Nauru, society is made up of juxtaposed, independent village communities, presided over by more or less equal chiefs who meet, when the need is felt, to decide collectively on the policy to follow. On the Caroline and Marshall islands on the other hand, power of decision is concentrated in the hands of a few aristocratic chieftains, marked by a strong hierarchical stratification founded on the mythological ancestry of clans of heroic or divine origin. The prime example of this system still survives in Pohnpei and above all in Yap, where the whole of the archipelago is divided into districts, in turn subdivided into subdistricts, each level being placed under the authority of titled men who, according to their social standing, have the right to receive tribute or perform rituals. Cross-observation of the geographical division of the different systems and historical chronology shows that the most elaborated societies arose in the most "civilized" zones of the west (for example Yap and its empire) and that the least developed were the prerogative of eastern societies that remained more "primitive".

*Dances in Micronesia,
particularly in Palau, Yap and Truk,
highlight ancient legends mingling graceful
movement with warlike violence.
Sung mimes celebrate brave deeds,
in particular those of women who have
always fought at the side of men.*

*At the dawn of time, all that existed was a single, underwater mountain, drowned in the infinite expanse of the primordial Ocean. The mountain contained the entire energy of the universe. At its summit was a tall tree, reduced to a simple and leafless trunk. On the day which had been planned by the gods, the base of the mountain rose up. A first god appeared whose name was Solal. Strong and dark as the angry wave, he climbed up the mountain. When he reached the summit, he uprooted the tree and cut it lengthways into several pieces which he made into an immense mast. Then he planted the mast into the rock and climbed up. When he had reached mid-way he emerged from the water. He stopped and created the earth which he made flat and desert-like. Then he continued to climb until he reached the top of the mast. There he created the sky which he fixed to the mast. Then he called Aluelop, he amongst his brothers who was born just after him. Light and clear as the sun, he immediately joined his elder brother who bestowed him with custody of the sky. Then Solal submerged under the surface of the Ocean, where he became the master of the nether world amidst his other brothers. For an infinite time, the upper and the nether world existed separately and nothing happened. But one day, bored in his heavenly kingdom, Aluelop invited Solal and proposed that they create new beings. Solal accepted. The two brothers therefore undertook to make and bring to life everything which today lives under the sea and in the air. Aluelop, whose head was full of ideas, imagined the various forms and Solal supplied the raw material of which there was an abundance. When the underwater plants and fish, the stars and birds had been installed either under the sea or in the air, the gods noticed that they had forgotten the earth. It has to be said that it was so small, lost as it was in the immensity of the Ocean and the sky! They placed numerous vegetable and animal species there. They made them all mortal, as they had decided that they would renew themselves, the older forms necessarily having to give way to the younger ones. Finally they invented man and woman to whom they entrusted the custody of their creation. As the mission of these guardians was an important one, they granted them immortality. Everything worked smoothly in the world which was thus created. In the sky, on the earth or in the Ocean, each vegetable or animal species was perfectly adapted to its living environment and multiplied. Only human beings seemed to experience some difficulty. Stiff and awkward, they could not swim like fish, fly like birds, nor run like dogs. Aluelop decided to send his son Lugeilan to help them. He came down from the sky amongst the human beings. He taught them to cultivate useful plants to feed themselves with. He taught them the art of tatooing and hairdressing so that they could distinguish themselves from the animals who could neither change nor embellish their appearance.*

*With the help of other gods, he showed them how to construct houses and dugout canoes. When he had accomplished his mission, he returned to the sky to his father Aluelop.*

*The god had, however, underestimated men, who were guileful and observant. They soon understood that the gods, Lugeilan foremost, considered them as their representatives on earth. Moreover, they were immortal, whereas everything that lived around them was destined to disappear. They concluded that they were superior to all other living beings. Their hearts swelled with an immense pride. They began cutting down trees indiscriminately, fishing and hunting for the simple pleasure of killing. They accumulated wealth and power. And, as they had numerous children, they ended up representing a force which worried the gods. Lugeilan was upset. His father, the powerful Aluelop, was angry. He removed immortality from men and subjected them to the common law of death.*

*Condemned to become wiser if they were to survive, men, now mortal, then began to look after their environment. Once his anger had subsided, Aluelop decided that it was time to bring them civilization. Having learned his lesson from the previous experience, he asked Lugeilan not to intervene personally with man, since they knew him only too well and, on seeing him, would be capable of attempting some new rebellion. He ordered him to unite with a mortal woman without her knowing it and to beget a being who would be both divine and human. Lugeilan chose a beautiful woman whom he fertilized during her sleep. Some time afterwards, the woman was seized with violent headaches. She lay down and went to*

# The legend of Lugeilan

*Micronesia is permanently aware that it is only an "accident" between the two infinities of the Sky and the Ocean. This myth from the central Caroline islands is a reminder.*

sleep. From her skull there emerged a luminous form which straightway took on a human appearance. This was Olofad, the mortal son of Lugeilan, who was to accomplish the mission entrusted to him by Aluelop. He found an earthly family. Wise and firm, he became the spiritual guide of his people in whom he instilled the main elements of culture, such as the art of telling tales, dancing and singing. As time went by, he felt so close to them that he contested the divine orders not to reveal too many secrets to man. Torn between his divine and human halves, Olofad finally chose the latter. He dared to go back up to the sky, confront the gods and make away with immortality so as to give it back once more to humans. He failed and was driven out of the heavenly kingdom. But, before leaving, he managed to steal a part of the sacred fire which he brought back to earth where it became the intelligence that was shared by men. As he still promised them immortality, the gods demanded Aluelop to punish him. The master of the heavens was about to strike the insolent Olofad when a group of men, jealous of the latter's popularity, led him into a trap, killed him and threw his body into the sea. Lugeilan pleaded with Solal and the other gods to be allowed to bring his son back to life. They accepted, but on condition that Olofad had nothing more to do with earth and men. After placing oblivion in his son's spirit, Lugeilan brought him back to life. Olofad settled in his father's celestial palace, where he led the life reserved for the gods. He never more thought about human beings who are still awaiting the return of the one who promised to deliver them from death.

*At dusk,*
*Tinian islanders make their way back to the shore*
*after collecting sea-shells at low tide.*

Western Micronesia has a marine surface area of over 5,000,000 km². It groups together the republic of Palau, the Commonwealth of the Northern Mariana Islands, the island of Guam and the Federated States of Micronesia. These archipelagoes are inhabited by populations whose authentically Micronesian ethnic and cultural characteristics are still clearly evident. Society is organized around an aristocracy dominated by important landowners whose authority is hereditary.

## PALAU, THE FORGOTTEN ARCHIPELAGO

The republic of Palau (or Belau) numbers approximately 16,500 inhabitants who generally carry on a traditional way of life which is, however, beginning to be influenced by Japan and the United States, particularly since the exceptional beauty of the underwater deeps has attracted tourists. The populations of Micronesian stock represent about one third of the islanders, another third being made up of other Oceanians or mixes from various origins. The rest is made up of Europeans and very strong Asian communities (Philippines, Indonesians, Taiwanese) who settled in the country at the end of the 19th Century, thereby modifying the ethnic identity of the native population in the most densely populated places. Palau is the last country under American trusteeship in the Pacific. In 1992, fourteen of the states which go to make up the republic accepted to transform the present status into a free association agreement with the U.S. The very unstable political situation in the territory has, however, brought a halt to the process. Palau is made up of approximately 350 islands of varying size and reefs which, for the most part, are grouped into two archipelagoes; to the north, Palaos with the large island of Babelthuap whose capital is Koror and, to the south, Sonsorol. The general alignment of the islands follows an arc from north-east to south-west which makes up the southern part of the underwater range bordering the Palau trench (over 27,900 feet deep). The total surface area of emerged lands is some 495 km² for a marine surface area of 630,000 km². Apart from

Babelthuap, whose massive, somewhat over-elevated structure recalls the morphology of the Pacific high islands after erosion has flattened their volcanic relief, the other islands have the classical structure of a coral atoll, of which Kayangel is an example, to the north of Babelthuap, and often presented by geographers as the perfect archetype. Despite being discovered early on by European navigators, the Palau archipelagoes have been completely forgotten by history, even if two world wars made brutal incursions there. Largely unaffected by international trade agreements, poorly assisted by the major powers who see no strategic or economic interest in them, often torn apart by violent local political struggles, they try to survive in a world which knows little about them.

## THE FEDERATED STATES OF MICRONESIA, A YOUNG NATION IN THE MAKING

The four Federated States of Micronesia make up a nation which has been independent since 1980. They occupy a marine surface area of 2,978,000 km², 700 km² of which is emerged land, made up of a multitude of often tiny atolls (over 2,200) scattered within four major groups, each of which has taken its name from the major island of the group. From west to east these are Yap (ex-western Carolinas), Truk (or Chuuk), Ponhpei (ex Ponape), Kosrae (or Kusaie, ex-eastern Carolinas). Yap, which was one of the first islands to appear, as attested by its geological formations, is based on a crystalline schist substratum. Flattened by strong erosion over the ages, its relief is in contrast to the mountainous and jagged relief of the other three main islands which are more recent. Generally the reliefs gain in height the further east one goes, which confirms the presence, doubtless far to the south-east, of the hot spot which gave rise to all these archipelagoes. The islands are surrounded by lagoons marked off by imposing barrier reefs. The one in Truk, which contains numerous secondary islands, is one of the largest in the Pacific. 129,000 people (including over 35% of authentic Micronesians, 20% of Polynesian mixture and 20% of various Oceanians) are unequally divided and live in the Federated States, the most populous of which is Ponhpei, seat of the Federal capital Kolonia).

Of all western Micronesia, it is in these four states that Micronesian identity bears its strongest stamp. Numerous pre-European traditions have been

*Unique in Micronesia,*
*the inhabitants of Yap*
*use rafts to get about*
*instead of boats*
*as on inland waterways.*

preserved despite the proselytism of Christian missionaries and Spanish, Japanese and American occupations.

In Yap, the old coinage in pierced stones and traditional clothing, particularly for men, are still retained.

In Truk and Kosrae, the ancient clan organisations of society and certain magic rituals have been partially maintained.

The presence of numerous Polynesian communities, certain of which arrived over 1,000 years ago,

has, however, changed the old Micronesian substrata in the eastern islands of Ponhpei and Kosrae, where Polynesians of pure stock represent over half the population.

After being admitted in 1991 to the U.N., the Federation has undergone a remarkable economic upturn, due in large part to considerable American investments whose most notable side effect is the rediscovered taste for numerous ancestral traditions. Undeniably this Micronesian nation has the wind in its sails.

▶

*Another strange customn*
*in Yap is the use*
*of the pierced stone.*
*Some weigh several tons.*
*With a 10-cm stone, people*
*can buy an animal, one of*
*2 m enables acquisition*
*of a whole village.*

## THE NORTHERN MARIANA ISLANDS AND GUAM: THE AMERICAN MODEL

The Mariana archipelago covers a marine surface area of 1,600,000 km², shared between the Commonwealth of the Northern Mariana Islands (1,460,000 km²), an independent state associated with the United States, and the large island of Guam (140,000 km²), which is a non-incorporated territory of the U.S. The surface area of emerged land is 477 km² for the former and 554 km² for the latter. The Commonwealth of the Northern Marianas is made up of fifteen medium-sized islands and several small inhabited islands of which the largest ones are Rota, Tinian and Saipan with the capital town of Chalan Kanoa, all three situated to the south of the archipelago. They stretch along an underwater arc in a north-south direction which, on its eastern side for 2,000 km, runs alongside the Mariana Trench, the deepest in the world with chasms over 36,000 feet. The southern extremity of this ocean range is marked by the large island of Guam whose capital is Agana.

The Northern Marianas and Guam are ancient volcanic islands, surrounded by barrier reefs. On account of the long process of erosion which they have undergone, relief is not very high. The highest point in the Northern Marianas is at Saipan, where Mount Topotchan reaches a mere 1,528 feet. In Guam, the only noteworthy relief is made up by hills to the south whose mean height is around 980 feet, with the highest point being Mount Lamlam, whose summit is at 1,328 feet. The Mariana islands number 30,000 inhabitants and Guam 129,000. Those of Micronesian stock are a minority (35% in the Northern Marianas and just over 10% in Guam), and Polynesians, Whites and Asians are largely dominant. The American influence is strongly felt everywhere. Even if, in the northern islands (Maug, Asuncion, Agrihan, Pagan), Micronesian traditions are still alive, in the south, on the other hand, and particularly in Guam, the American way of life has replaced old customs in a population that has become very westernized and urbanized.

Modernisation has brought with it a strong influx of communities of European and Asian stock. The divide between rich and poor in the Micronesian community is, however, ever widening as, cut off from their cultural origins, they are unable to choose between a risky return to grass roots and a headlong lurch into the lap of the Americans.

*Chewing a betel nut still remains
one of the favourite passtimes of men.*

*A magnificent specimen
of a tulip tree.
Imported by Europeans,
the tree has spread
throughout the Pacific.*

▶

*The western archipelagoes of the Marianas and the Federated States house
significant historical remains,
some of which date back to the Neolithic period.
All bear witness to a very ancient tradition of a powerful centralized state.*

Two men guard the entrance to the communal house.
Typical of Micronesian culture, these large buildings
serve as meeting places for the periodic gatherings
of clan chiefs and various ceremonies.

*The population of Guam,*
*the most populous island of the Marianas,*
*is concentrated along a coastal strip.*
*The interior is a succession of high hills*
*which are totally uninhabited.*

◄

*Daily life goes on at the slow and even pace of nature*
*which gives the islanders all they want,*
*for example in the Palaos, Marianas or Kosrae.*

*Some of the numerous small islands, for the most part inhabited,*
*that go to make up the vast coral crown surrounding the atoll of Tarawa in Kiribati.*

The total marine surface area of eastern Micronesia is the largest in the Pacific and covers some 5,870,000 km². It includes the republics of the Marshall islands, Nauru and Kiribati. The populations are further removed from the original Micronesian type as the area has, for some two thousand years, seen numerous migrations, mainly Polynesian, which explains the significant proportion of the latter and sometimes almost their entire domination in some archipelagoes. The village community is dominated by the exogamous group of relations linked by the cult of ancestry and by the various local confraternities whose role is to monitor how society functions and regulate ritual, inter-clan exchanges.

## THE MARSHALL ISLANDS, OR THE HISTORY OF A CULTURAL RESISTANCE

The republic of the Marshall islands, which became an independent state in 1979, has been linked by a treaty of free association with the U.S. since 1986. It covers a marine surface area of 2,130,000 km², of which 181 km² is emerged land. It is made up of over 1,200 islands of varying sizes which for the most part follow two alignments of atolls in a north-west to south-easterly direction and situated in a complex, even anarchic pattern above the long underwater Marshall-Gilbert-Ellice range. There is the group of eighteen westerly atolls of Ralik (or islands of the Setting Sun) and that of the sixteen atolls of Ratak (or islands of the Rising Sun), including Majuro with the capital Uliga. All these islands are ancient coral formations situated around a central lagoon and are no more than 13 feet above sea level. The Marshall lagoons are the largest in the world, and it is not uncommon to find some that measure 100 km in diameter. Kwajalein, the largest in the Ralik group alone covers a marine surface area of 2,300 km².

The population of the Marshall islands is 41,600 inhabitants, most of whom are made up of Micronesians and Polynesians who together, and in approximately equal proportions, form 75% of the total population. There are also Melanesian and Asiatic communities living in the Marshalls. Unlike what happened in other Micronesian archi-

# 5
## 3

# THE MARSHALL ISLANDS, NAURU & KIRIBATI

### (EASTERN MICRONESIA)

pelagoes, mixing with Whites and Asians in particular has been uncommon. The Polynesian contribution to the Micronesian stock has been particularly strong in the atolls of the east and the south. The geographical position of the Marshall islands constitutes an important strategical pivot for the Americans who are present in all the atolls, in particular those of the centre and the north, where they have installed military bases, in Kwajalein for example. Access to others, such as Bikini or Eniwetok, which served as theatres for nuclear testing, has for a long time been prohibited, even to Micronesians. Vegetation is relatively poor, with the exception of abundant coconut trees and pandanus. In the northern atolls, there are but a few halophilous plants. In the south, useful plants (taroes, yams, breadfruit and cocoa trees) are grown throughout the year.

In addition to the Marshall islands, the United States also administer other small Micronesian islands that were formerly uninhabited, situated outside eastern Micronesian limits and which have been entrusted to one of the armed forces: Wake island (7.8 km²) to the Air Force, Johnston (2 km²) to the Army, Midway (5.2 km²) to the Navy. Some are private property such as Palmyra, or are uninhabited, such as Kingman, Jarvis, Howland and Baker. Two are Anglo-American condimiums, Canton and Enderbury, in the Phoenix archipelago.

## NAURU, RICH MICRONESIA PEOPLED BY POLYNESIANS

Discovered in 1798 by the English captain Fearn, Nauru was annexed by Germany in 1888 before being occupied by the Australians during the First World War, then by the Japanese during the Second.

In 1968, it became the independent republic of Nauru within the British Commonwealth. It is situated to the west of the Gilbert islands, near to the Equator and has a marine surface area of 320,000 km². It is made up of an atoll of 22 km² with one large island, surrounded by a coral barrier reef. The island, with its capital Yaren, is situated on a relief, isolated on the eastern fringe from the numerous minor folds of the Solomon

*Despite the apparent frailty of their black, triangular sails,*
*characteristic of the Buariki islands,*
*the fishing boats prove to be particularly efficient even during stormy weather.*

shelf. It is like a vast table of coral limestone, which is never higher than 150 feet in the centre and which gradually slopes down to a narrow, very fertile coastal plain. With the exception of this plain, almost all of the island is covered by an immense deposit of phosphates. Nauru has the highest population density in the Pacific, with 380 inhabitants per km². There are 9,200 people on the island, 65% of which are Polynesians from all horizons. Half the inhabitants are Naurus, a term which designates mixes of Polynesians and Malaysians or Indonesians. Other Polynesians from Tuvalu, Wallis and Futuna and the Gilbert islands, constitute 18% of the population. The rest is made up of authentic Micronesians (12%), Chinese from Hong Kong and Whites. The considerable income derived from phosphates has assured a high general standard of living, but the natives seem to resist fairly effortlessly the various attractions and temptations of western civilization. On "modern" Nauru, which has frequent contacts with Australia, New Zealand, Japan and the United Kingdom, the most traditional ancestral values may still paradoxically be found, deeply rooted into customs and mentalities, such as the ritual belonging to clans and the family handing-down of original myths.

## KIRIBATI: THE ABSOLUTE 'TWIXT SKY AND OCEAN

Crossed by the Equator in its northern part, the republic of Kiribati is situated in the centre of the Pacific. With a marine surface area of over 3,550,000 km², it is one of the most extensive states in the Pacific. The overall surface area of emerged land is, however, only 728 km².

Kiribati is made up of the large island of Banaba (or Ocean island), thirty-two atolls spread over three archipelagoes, Gilbert, Phoenix and Line and a multitude of uninhabited small islands and reefs. The Gilbert island group has sixteen atolls, including Tarawa, the largest where the capital of Bairiki is situated. The Phoenix archipelago groups together eight atolls, and Line, to which eight of the eleven islands belong (equitorial Sporades) and three of which belong to the United States.

*Cut off from the outside world, the eastern Micronesian islanders are poor. They patch up their boats with any material they can find in the ocean.*

*The island of Buota is renowned*
*for the traditional architecture of its villages,*
*its refined art and the quality of its dances.*

The origin, and therefore the structure, of Banaba island is identical to that of Nauru, from which it is only a hundred or so kilometres away. Like Nauru, it comes from an isolated relief in the shape of a vast coral limestone table, whose height varies from 65 to 130 feet above sea-level. Its ground also contains significant deposits of phosphates, today practically exhausted. The atolls, on the other hand, have almost all the same shape: a vast inner lagoon marked off by a coral island belt - mean height between 6 and 12 feet. Their alignment is north-west to south-east, corresponding to underwater volcanic chains. The case

of the islanders who have a growing birthrate. Except on the island of Banaba where market-gardening and fruit-growing abound, the land is poor and practically the only crops which can be grown are coconut and its by-products (copra), pandanus and taro. The general standard of living is quite low, keeping the inhabitants in a state of semi-destitution, confirming the ancient legends which say that their archipelago was only a sort of "accident" that had occurred 'twixt sky and ocean. Off the beaten trade and tourist tracks, the natives of Kiribati have easily retained the ancient way of life, founded on the social structure of clans and

*The former contacts between western Micronesians and Polynesians are clearly demonstrated in this Canton family, in the Phoenix islands, and this young girl from Majuro, in the Marshall islands.*

▶

*The fishermen from Kiribati are used to lashing the planks of their boats with strong rope made from palm fibres.*

of the Phoenix islands poses some problems insofar as geologists have not yet determined whether their origin is due to the fact that they belong to an underwater fold or to the emergence of isolated reliefs. Kiribati has a total population of 74,000 inhabitants, 42% of which are Micronesians, 28% pure Polynesians and 30% mixes of the two communities. The remaining 2% is made up of Europeans, Asians and other Oceanians. Many islands are uninhabited and, of the others, only twenty are so permanently, including the Gilbert islands, where the majority of the population is concentrated, Canton (one of the Phoenix islands), three of the Line atolls (Kirimanti or Christmas islands, Teraina and Tabuaeran) and Banaba island. The population is of Micronesian stock in Banaba and the Gilbert islands, and Polynesian in the other atolls.

Agriculture is hardly sufficient to meet the needs

natural rhythms. Seasons, cyclones, bird migrations, movement of fish shoals - all these condition the activities of hunting and fishing.

The successive colonisations which they underwent from the 18th Century onwards did not disturb their way of life. At most, the odd missionary

managed to have them accept a syncretism of ancient cults and Christianity. Even the Second World War and its brutal intrusion into the territory (the Battle of Tarawa in 1943 was one of the climaxes of the war between Japanese and Americans) just seems like a past mishap today, were it not for the few shells of Japanese war engines rusting away on the beaches of Tarawa amidst general indifference.

*"Maneaba" are present in most of the eastern archipelagoes. These large community houses, built on "magic" sites house political meetings and celebrations.*

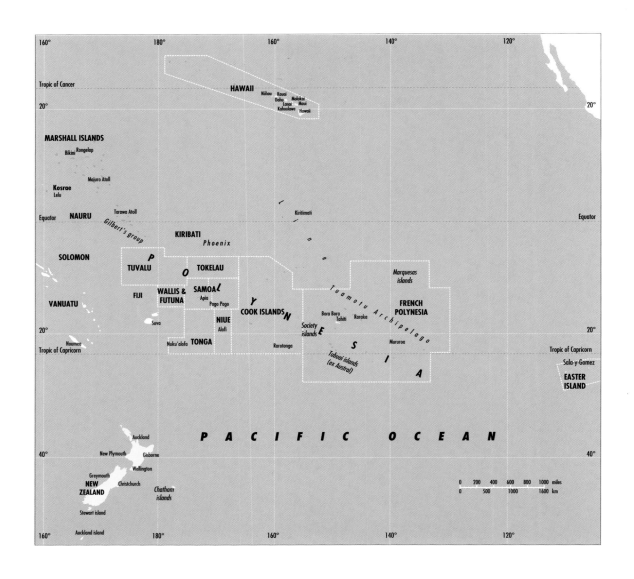

Tropic of Cancer

HAWAII
Niihau Kauai
Oahu Molokai
Lanai Maui
Kahoolawe Hawaii

MARSHALL ISLANDS
Bikini Rongelap

Majuro Atoll

Kosrae
Lelu

Tarawa Atoll

Kiritimati

Equator                    NAURU                                                                                                                Equator

Gilbert's group

KIRIBATI
Phoenix

SOLOMON                                                    P

TUVALU                O          TOKELAU

Marquesas
islands

FIJI        WALLIS &    SAMOA
            FUTUNA      Apia
                                                    Y

Tuamotu Archipelago

VANUATU                                     Pago Pago

                                    COOK ISLANDS   N        Bora Bora    Raraka
                                                            Tahiti                FRENCH
                        Suva                                                      POLYNESIA

                                    NIUE
                                    Alofi                        Society
                                                                islands        E
20°                                                                                              S              20°
            Noumea         Nuku'alofa    TONGA                                                   I
Tropic of Capricorn                                    Raratonga        Tabuai islands
                                                                        (ex Austral)                    A          Sala-y-Gomez

                                                                                                              EASTER
                                                                                                              ISLAND
                                                                                    Mururoa

PACIFIC    OCEAN

                    Auckland
NEW Plymouth    Gisborne

            Wellington
Greymouth
NEW                 Christchurch    Chatham
ZEALAND                             islands

Stewart island

Auckland island

# 6

## 1

# POLYNESIA

Polynesia, or "numerous islands" (from the Greek *polu* "many" and *nesos* "island") owes its name to the vast number of islands that go to make it up. These are scattered over an immense triangle in the central and eastern Pacific, either side of the equator, the three corners of the triangle being formed by the Hawaiian islands to the north, Easter island to the east and New Zealand to the south-west. Polynesia is divided into eighteen political entities. Three are totally independent nations, seven are semi-autonomous and associated with other major countries, and eight are territories and isolated islands belonging to a third country, generally the former colonial power. The former include the kingdom of Tonga which obtained its independence from the United Kingdom in 1970, Tuvalu (ex-Ellice islands) which gained its independence from the United Kingdom in 1978 and the Western Samoa islands which obtained independence from New Zealand in 1962. To the second category belong the Eastern Samoa islands and Guam which are non-incorporated U.S. territories, Niue and the Cook islands which

are autonomous states associated with New Zealand, Tokelau which is a New Zealand overseas territory, and Wallis and Futuna which are French overseas territories. The third category groups together numerous islands, the main ones being Sala y Gomez, Juan Fernandez and Easter island which belong to Chile, the Galapagos and Gigedos islands which are Mexican, the Coral Sea Territory, Lord Howe and Norfolk islands which are under Australian administration, the Hawaiian islands and various isolated islands such as Midway, Wake, Johnston, Palmyra, Howland, Baker, Jarvis and Kingman which are attached to the United States, the Antipodes islands, Kermadec, Chatman, Bounty, Auckland and Campbell which are New Zealand dependencies and finally Pitcairn island which is the last British colony in the Pacific.

## A MYRIAD OF VOLCANIC AND CORAL FORMATIONS

Like Micronesia, Polynesia is part of the true Ocean, with the exception of New Zealand which is a case apart. Like the majority of Oceania, the numerous Polynesian archipelagoes owe their existence to the immense Darwin fold that undergoes tectonic plate movements and hot-spot activity. The shelves have been subjected to a succession of strong orogenic thrusts, followed in the Cenozoic period by significant subsidence movements which first of all brought about the appearance then the partial disappearance of the old archipelagoes. Most Polynesian archipelagoes are the emerged summits of underwater volcanic ranges with an abundance of basalts from the Tertiary, but particularly the Quaternary periods, and Eocene limestone. The islands are often surrounded by barrier reefs. In places where volcanic formations disappeared underwater, after erosion, then collapsed on account of the fact that, following crustal plate movement, they were cut off from the hot-spot, the only visible surface remains are the coral crowns which built up on their slopes; in a word, the atolls.

## A TROPICAL CLIMATE WITH POOR FLORA AND FAUNA

Again with the exception of New Zealand, the climate is of a tropical type. The fact that most of the islands are situated in the tropical zone of the Southern Hemisphere means that there is hardly any temperature variation and that rainfall is relatively moderate, albeit regular. Dragged into tropical convergence atmospheric currents, air masses go from the Tropic of Capricorn to the

*On the high islands,*
*the reliefs of eastern windward slopes retain the clouds*
*with consequent heavy rainfall.*

◀

*In the Society archipelago,*
*the island of Raiatea is a sacred land for Tahitians,*
*and is considered to be the cradle of their civilization.*

Equator, then, taking a left turn, give rise to the trade winds which blow permanently from April to November, cooling the temperature which hardly varies from 26°C throughout the year. The rains, which fall especially in summer from December to March, are not very abundant on the low islands and the western slopes of high islands, unexposed to ocean winds. On the other hand, eastern mountain slopes receive much more rain, up to 3,000mm per year. On account of its geographical situation to the north-east, the Hawaiian archipelago has even more rainfall. As for the Chilean and Mexican islands to the east, their climates are specific, often very wet and with significant temperature ranges on account of proximity with the American mainland and the presence of cold oceanic currents. Sometimes the Polynesian zone is the scene of violent cyclones between November and March, affecting western islands in particular, such as Samoa, Tuvalu, Wallis and Futuna but sparing those situated near to the Equator and New Zealand which is too low down in the Southern Hemisphere. They are also exceptional in French Polynesia and Hawaii.

The flora is typical of the Indo-Pacific intertropical zone and follows the general pattern, becoming increasingly poor the further east one travels. The Polynesian islands are covered with a luxuriant vegetation, which seems to be in contradiction with the extreme sparseness of species, most of the 200 of which that have been indexed are indigenous, with only twenty or so naturally abundant. In the atolls and the low parts of the high islands, mangroves, pandanus and coconut trees are the most common species. The mountain slopes of the high islands are covered in conifers, and, to a lesser degree, in oak and beech. The action of man who has introduced a considerable stock of useful plants (yams, taroes, sweet potatoes, banana, coffee and citrus trees) was decisive for the environment which it enriched but at the same time significantly changed. Thus the latania and the guava trees have become veritable scourges in Tahiti.

Fauna is typically Oceanian. Before the arrival of man who first brought in pigs, rats, dogs then sheep, cattle, horses, deer and poultry, no superior mammal lived in the Polynesian archipelagoes, except perhaps for a variety of bat. Other species are poorly represented. There are no snakes and only a few tortoises and lizards are to be found. Insects are also rare. Although the bird population is better represented, it is on the whole poor and most species live off the sea. The most common are terns, noddies, gannets and frigates. Amongst

*The southern coast of Savaii in Western Samoa is a succession of black basalt blocks.*

landbirds can be found reef egrets, pigeon-parrots and various doves. Here also, man altered the environment, when 17th Century navigators introduced the Spice island blackbird which has developed to such an extent that it is threatening the original birdlife balance.

## POPULATIONS WHICH HAVE BECOME VICTIMS OF THEIR REPUTATION

Traditionally, Polynesian populations live from and for the ocean, with which they have a quasi-carnal relationship. Inventors of the outrigger dugout canoe and the *katamaran*, the islanders have an innate sense of navigation which they ally with a perfect knowledge of the stars, winds and sea currents. But they have also become farmers who can get the best out of a generally unfertile soil. They grow taroes, yams, citrus fruits and various vegetables. The pandanus and the coconut tree give by-products which are used each day and which, when commercialized, provide a significant source of income.

Polynesian societies are much larger and better structured than those in Melanesia and Micronesia.

Before the arrival of Europeans, there were already several thousand inhabitants in Tahiti and Somoa and tens of thousands in Tonga and Hawaii. These large socio-political entities were based on a system of chieftains which, for the most part, still functions today. Linearity is on either the father's or the mother's side and the hierarchical structure strong in a society where heredity is the chieftan rule. It was formerly in the hands of a noble aristocracy and priests who exerted an absolute power over their communities. Combatted by Europeans, this character has survived in the form of families of eminent citizens who, through their ancient ancestry, prestige and wealth enjoy real power. Polynesia has had its powerful kings and queens, and today it is the clan heads who actually run the different archipelagoes. The notion of title is capital as this confers authority on its owner and brings the respect of others. One of the particularities of Polynesia is that such title is not simply hereditary but can be acquired by merit or alliance with a man or marriage with a woman who already possess it. The accumulation of titles gives a power which is directly proportional to the number of such titles. Thus it is that the Polynesian islands are today held by a handful of families who have often "bought" a part of their titles over the ages.

*A young woman from Tonga,*
*with the traditional tavala around her waist,*
*weaves a mat for lying down.*

*The healthy beauty of island women,*
*here an inhabitant of Moorea, has fascinated foreign visitors*
*for almost three centuries.*

Europeans have been marked by Polynesians more than any other Oceanian population. The beauty of the islands, the natural grace of the islanders, the warm nonchalance of the way of life led successive discoverers to confer an idyllic image on the natives. Thus Polynesia became a land of dreams, a sort of paradise regained where life was sweet. But the influx of visitors and traders which followed has destroyed local societies much more than it has helped them. Often

considered as "nice natives" who do not really need to work, Polynesians have spent a long time battling for recognition of their cultural identity. Today still, the tenacious myth still hounds them amidst an often iconoclastic tourism.

*The natural environment has been preserved. Flowers -here a variety of hibiscus- and birds -here a red-clawed gannet- abound.*

*Sitting in the shade of his fale, a Samoan from Malua Faleula makes celebration garlands.*

*In the darkness of an absolute night, Rangi, the male sky, and Papa, the female earth, put an end to the Void by giving it a top and a bottom. Then they united and, locked in their embrace, remained closely entwined. They gave birth to many sons. The most powerful were called Tu, god of war, Tawhiri, lord of winds and storms, Rongo, master of Peace and agriculture, Haumia, protector of ungrown food, Tangaroa, ruler of the ocean, and Tane, sovereign of the forests. But these gods could hardly breathe or move. Neither could they see anything. They were wedged between their parents' bodies who remained eternally in each other's arms, maintaining a total and permanent night. The sons therefore resolved to get together so as to solve the situation. With the exception of Tawhiri who refused to speak, they all agreed that Rangi and Papa should be separated so as to create the indispensable vital space. Tu, the most violent of the gods, proposed that their parents should purely and simply be killed. Tawhiri indignantly objected to this project. Tane then proposed that they should be separated gently. His brothers approved, but Tawhiri said that in his opinion nothing should be changed in the divine order and that if Rangi and Papa had chosen to remain entwined, no one had the right to disturb them. Despite his opposition, the gods decided to take up Tane's proposal. Furious, Tawhiri warned that he would allow no one to disturb the peace of his parents and left the assembly.*

*Heedless of his brother's threats, Tane set about the task. Using his body as a lever, he braced himself against those of Rangi and Papa and succeeded in separating them. Light immediately flooded in, illuminating the world. The other gods applauded. With his arms stretched out over his head, Tane held Rangi in the air. He asked his brothers to lower Papa so as to increase the space. They then began to trample on Papa. So violently did they strike their mother's body that they pushed practically all of her below the surface of the water. Just a few parts remained visible here and there. These are the islands. The young gods gave vent to their joy. But this did not last long. Roaring with anger, Tawhiri, crossed the space in a single leap to rejoin his father and, from up on high, liberated the army of winds and storms on his brothers.*

*Panic-stricken, all the gods fled, leaving the fiery Tu alone to face this fearsome troupe. The powerful god of war resisted valliantly against their onslaught, finally discouraging them and forcing them to withdraw. Victory did not, however, make his heart joyous, so full was it of bitterness. His brothers had forsaken him in a cowardly manner at the very moment of danger. He resolved to take his vengeance and punish them. Thus began a long war between the gods which shook the world and almost destroyed it. Tu defied and vanquished each of his brothers whom he chained up one after the other. Soon only Tawhiri and Tane were left. Tawhiri was unable to resist for long the fury of Tu who tied him up head downwards. The god of war then turned to Tane. The two brothers confronted each other in the middle of the sky. Tu had strength but Tane guile. After a terrible combat, Tane emerged victorious. He exiled Tu for ever to the earth and freed his brothers with whom he entrusted several missions. Then he reconciled with Tawhiri and followed him up to the sky. There he undertook to console his father, grey and covered with sad clouds and grieved at being separated from his wife. Tane explained why he and his brothers had been forced to act thus. In order to obtain forgiveness and bring back joy to his father's heart, he placed the sun on Rangi's head and fixed the moon to his brow. He then unfurled an immense cloak on his back onto which he had attached thousands of stars which shone like so many precious stones. Rangi's face lit up. It became radiant blue and the clouds disappeared.*

*With the sky having regained its serenity, Tane thought that it was time to devote himself to his mother Papa. He asked her what she would like. She said that she would like to have new children. Seeing that Tane was perplexed, she advised him to unite with already existing female entities. He obeyed. His multiple unions with such entities gave birth to all sorts of new stones, trees, plants and unknown animals. But none satisfied either Papa or Tane. They wanted a completely new being which would honour them and be in their image. Following his mother's indications, the god first went to the ocean's edge, where there was a pure river she had told him of. He mixed the sand of the former with the clay of the latter and pugged them for a long time. When he had obtained an*

# The legend of Tane

*The cosmogonical myth can be found throughout Polynesia. Its particular genius is that it succeeds in bringing about a perfect blend of the abstract, the marvelous and the everyday.*

*even compound, he called his brothers and asked them to help him model it in the image of their mother. Some saw to giving it its general shape, others added muscles and blood. When the body was finished, Tane spread himself over it and breathed into its mouth. The form came to life. The god who had never had any sexual experience, did not know how to fertilize it. His clumsy attempts only succeeded in damaging his companion, whose eyes filled with tears, her nose with mucus, her ears with wax and her armpits with sweat. The god finally found her vagina and coupled with her. From their union was born a daughter whom they called Hine.*

*When she reached womanhood, Tane married her. She gave him many children. But she constantly tried to discover the secret of her origins. One day she learnt that her husband was also her father. Grief-stricken by the incest which was the origin of the human race, Hine fled underground to hide her shame.*

*There she became queen of Rarohenga, the nether kingdom, and was known as Hine nui te po, goddess of death. Intent on taking her vengeance on Tane, she undertook to attract the fruits of their union, as well as their descendants, into her realm.*

*Thus it is that all men and women must inevitably, one day or another, descend to the netherworld...*

*The often rough waters which wash the eastern beaches of black volcanic sand,
store a host of fish of which the villagers take advantage.*

The archipelagoes of Tuvalu, Tokelau, Niue, Wallis and Futuna are situated around the Samoa islands with which they make up the north-west Polynesian group. This zone is considered by many as the first true "matrix" of the Polynesian nation, not simply in accordance with legends which consider it the centre of Polynesia but also in the light of discoveries which confirm its ethnic and cultural antecedence.

## SAMOA: TRADITIONS AND MODERNISM

The archipelago of Samoa is politically divided between the independent state (since 1962) of Western Samoa which is part of the British Commonwealth and the autonomous, non-incorporated territory of Eastern Samoa attached to the United States in 1899. The total marine surface area is 510,000 km², of which 120,000 km² for Western Samoa and 390,000 km² for its eastern counterparts. The former are made up of two main islands, Upolu, with the capital Apia and Savaii, and two minor islands, Apolima and Manono together with small uninhabited islands. The total landmass surface area is 2,842 km². American Samoa has a main island, Tutuila, with the capital Pago Pago, the Manua island group which includes the islands of Tau, Ofu and Olosega, the eastern Rose atoll and Swains island, situated 300 km to the north. Total island surface area is 200 km².

### A MOUNTAINOUS GROUP CENTERED IN AN AREA OF STRONG VOLCANIC ACTIVITY

Separated by a strait, 75 kms at its widest point, the two Samoan states are part of the same mountainous alignment. Of volcanic origin, the two main islands are the emerged cones of a high underwater chain made up of andesites and basalts dating from the Miocene and Pliocene periods. Particularly in its western half, this substratum has undergone strong volcanic activity linked to an abundant network of underwater fractures along a south-east to north-west axis. The morphology of the Western Samoan mountainous alignment which is higher and less eroded to the east (Mount Silisili in Savaii peaks

# 6
---
## 2

# THE ISLANDS OF SAMOA, TOKELAU, TUVALU, WALLIS & FUTUNA

at 6,048 feet) than in the west (Fito and Vaaifetu reach only 3,608 feet) leads us to think that underwater eruptions were centered at a hot-spot to the east, along a fracture on the ocean bed. This hypothesis is confirmed by the identical morphological structure of Eastern Samoa which is not as high (the Tau cone peaks at only 3,053 feet) and is more eroded because it corresponds to the most ancient part of the underwater chain that gave rise to the Samoan group as a whole. Following the intense volcanic activity of the Quaternary period, there followed a relatively stable period of statis, but post-volcanic phenomena are still very much present in Savaii, where a crater opened in the side of the Matanavu volcano, from where there flowed an immense 12km-long and 300m-wide river of lava.

### A SUCCESSION OF FOREIGN OCCUPATIONS

The presence of archeological sites dating from the end of the second millenium BC and the discovery of large monuments such as the "pyramid" of Savaii, lead one to think that Samoa, together with Tonga, are the oldest inhabited sites of Polynesia. Discovered in 1722 by the Dutchman Roggeveen, the islands were not colonized until the middle of the 19ᵗʰ Century, when they became the centre of a dispute between England, Germany and the United States who all vied for mastery of this remarkable strategic point right in the middle of the Pacific. The Berlin conference of 1889 first of all mutually entrusted the administration of the archipelago to the three rival powers. The result was an even greater struggle for influence. Ten years later a new treaty granted the land to the west of the 171st meridian to Germany and those situated to the east to the United States. In 1914, under pretext of freeing the islands from the German yoke, New Zealand sent troops into the archipelago.

At the end of the Second World War, Western Samoa was trusted to New Zealand who granted it independence in 1962. Although enjoying a certain autonomy, Eastern Samoa remained the property of the Americans. The difference between the two parts of the archipelago has

*The Samoan "fale" does not have any walls.*
*To sleep or when the wind is too strong,*
*palm blinds woven by girls are stretched between the pillars that uphold the thatched roof.*

*Sweet potatoes,*
*yams and taroes form the staple diet*
*and a digging stick is still commonly used.*

*Samoa, and in particular the island of Upolu,*
*has superb specimens of banyans*
*with their long aerial roots.*

continued to increase since then. The traditional system of life of the Western Samoans is contrasted by the American way of life of their eastern counterparts. This phenomenon is reflected by the very make-up of the two populations. In Western Samoa, 88% of the 158,000 inhabitants are Polynesian, only 2% European and the remaining 10% made up by Melanesians and Euronesians (White and Polynesian mix). On the other hand, almost 60% of the 38,000 Eastern Samoans are Europeans or Euronesians. The ancient way of life has remained prevalent in the west, where the villagers, dressed in traditional clothes most of the time, follow old community laws. The traditional unwalled *fales* go with an economy founded on fishing and agriculture. To the east, the inhabitants, dressed mostly after the American fashion, live more and more in solid constructions and work in factories. Although they have gained a definite advantage from an economic point of view, they have to a large extent lost the Polynesian soul that goes to make up the charm of their western cousins.

## TOKELAU, THE ARCHIPELAGO WITH NO HISTORY

The Tokelau (or Union) islands are situated approximately 500 kms north of Samoa.

They are a sort of succession, stretching from north-west to south-east, of three small atolls, made up of coral islands whose total surface area is no more than 10 km² and which are centered in a marine area of 290,000 km².

Their names are Atafu (2 km²), Fakaofo (2.6 km²) and Nukunonu (5.5 km²) where about 1,700 Polynesians live and which make up the overseas territory of Tokelau administered by New Zealand. Noted but not explored, they were annexed in the 19th Century by the British who almost never set foot on the islands, and were constantly cut off from the rest of the world on account of their remoteness and size. Practically forgotten during the period of colonization, which meant that their inhabitants were spared the sad fate of the rest of the Oceanians, they entered the 20th Century by the back door. Today there is no aerodrome, road or hotel. Even the administrative capital is not on the archipelago but at Apia, in Western Samoa. Nature has remained intact and the natives live almost like their ancestors two centuries ago, from fishing and crafts. Social life is based on a traditional clan structure and the absolute respect of community decisions.

# TUVALU,
## A YOUNG OVERPOPULATED STATE

The Tuvalu islands (ex-Ellice islands) were granted independence by the United Kingdom in 1978, but are still part of the British Commonwealth. The territorial waters of the young state cover 900,000 km² and landmass is only 26 km². 12,000 islanders live in close proximity with each other and represent the densest

population in Oceania, over 460 inhabitants per km², spread over nine coral atolls (one of which is uninhabited). From north-west to south-east, Nanumea, Nanumanga, Niutao, Nui, Vaitupu, Nukufetau, Funafuti, where the capital of Vaiaku is situated, Nukulaelae and Niulakita between which emerge the reefs of Kosciusko Bank. These low coral atolls (mean height 10 feet) are the southerly extension of the Gilbert islands. They succeed each other at the summit of the long underwater chain called Marshall-Gilbert-Ellice. Like the Gilbert islands, the Tuvalu are made up of volcanic rocks (basalts) that date essentially from the Quaternary period and of coral formations, the most ancient of which, of Eocene limestone, have been noted in Funafuti.

*Despite the omnipresent American way of life in Eastern Samoa, the "fa'a samoa" -in the manner of our fathers- still remains the general reference.*

The Tuvalu islands were discovered in 1568 by the Spaniard Pendana. They were not particularly colonized until the 19th Century when the inhabitants were used as labour in the mines and plantations of South America, Australia and Oceania. The action of the missionaries was also a key one, breaking up the ancient structures. The native population diminished by almost two thirds. The archipelago became known as the Ellice islands when they were annexed by the British Crown in 1877. They were then attached to the Gilbert islands, from which they decided to separate after the referendum of 1974. In 1977, they changed their name to Tuvalu, which means "eight (inhabited atolls) united". The great majority of inhabitants of Tuvalu are Polynesian, making up 91% of the population. The rest is made up of Euronesians (6%), miscellaneous Oceanians (2%) and Whites (1%). The fact that the atolls are extremely scattered does not enable them to have a feeling of national belonging. With the exception of Fanafuti which is linked with the outside world by an aerodrome and a trading port, the different communities, isolated on their islands, continue to live in accordance with ancestral traditions. Fishing, agriculture and crafts provide minimal resources. Many islanders are leaving the country, going in particular to Nauru and Kiribati to work and improve their standard of living which is one of the lowest in the world.

## WALLIS AND FUTUNA, TWO VERY DIFFERENT VOLCANIC ISLANDS

The overseas French Territory of Wallis & Futuna (or Horn) is situated between the Melanesian islands of Fiji and the Polynesian islands of Samoa. It is made up of two archipelagoes, with a total surface area of 255 km² situated in 300,000 km² of ocean and which are in fact the emerged summits of the Marṣhall-Gilbert-Ellice chain. Despite having a common origin, their aspect is quite different. Whilst Wallis is a welcoming "paradise" island, Futuna is harsh and mountainous. The archipelago of Wallis (96 km²) includes the main island of Uvea and the capital Mata Utu, the two small islands of Faioa and Nukuatea, as well as several reefs... The archipelago of Futuna (159 km²) is made up of two islands, Futuna and Alofi. The structure of the main islands of the two groups is identical: a low, volcanic cone (the highest point in Uvea is only 465 feet) surrounded by a barrier reef. Volcanic and limestone formations are the same as those on other archipelagoes in the Marṣhall-Gilbert-Ellice chain.

There are 15,200 inhabitants on Wallis and Futuna, 98% of which are of Polynesian stock, with an occasional, doubtless ancient, Melanesian influence. The rest of the population is made up of Europeans and other Oceanians.

Inhabited by Polynesians since the first millenium, the two archipelagoes were colonized by Fijians in the 12th Century. In the 17th Century, Futuna was discovered by the Dutchmen Lemaire and Schouten who called it Horn. A century later, the Englishman Wallis landed on the other group and gave it his name. Contacts with the local population were quite good and allowed the archipelagoes to be evangilized, notably by the Marists who set up a veritable theocracy. Placed under French protectorate at the end of the 19th Century and after a brief American occupation during the Second World War, the Wallis and Futuna islands became a French overseas Territory in 1961. The islanders are all today officially catholic. Nevertheless, despite an omnipresent French administration, the ancient customs have been relatively well preserved.

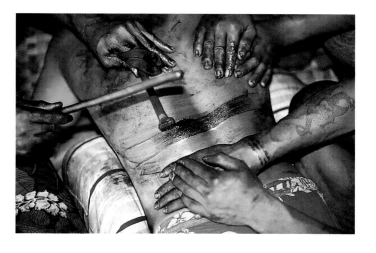

*Samoan tatoos
are amongst the most famous
in the Polynesian world.
The men's always represent
the prows of a boat,
in a stylized motif
(around the waist),
the fale (on the hips),
marine animals
(from the buttocks to the knees).
A complete tatooing
is a week's painful ordeal.*

▶

*An image of three men
picking up shells
on Falalupo beach at low tide
seems to come from the past.*

*Inhabitants on the island of Apolima strike the water
and gradually close in their boats
to encircle and trap the fish.*

*A young islander from Uvea
in the Wallis archipelago.*

*The atoll of Fanafuti,
the largest in Tuvalu,
stretches for some
thirty kilometres.
Slow and peaceful,
daily life is centered around
fishing-related activities.*

*On a warm southern-hemisphere winter's evening,*
*a fisherman returns to Nomuka, in the Ha'apai group.*

The Tonga islands together with Niue make up South West Polynesia. For over one thousand years, the different Tongan dynasties have reigned over an immense geographical zone which they have dominated without partition from political, economic and cultural points of view. The Tongan zone, to which Niue belongs and which was peopled by emigrants from Tongatapu, was inhabited by the first Polynesian navigators, doubtless originating from Samoa at the beginning of the Christian era.

## TONGA, THE LAST KINGDOM OF THE PACIFIC

The archipelago of the Tonga islands covers a marine surface area of 700,000 km², of which 700 km² is landmass. It is made up of two island garlands aligned parallel to each other on an ocean shelf that separates the Tonga Trench to the east, one of the deepest in the world (35,095 feet), from the Lau basin to the west.

### VOLCANOES AND LOW ISLANDS

The western alignment is made up of a main island, Tofua, and ten or so small islands, some of which are geological curiosities, such as Fonuafo'ou (or Falcon Bank) to the south, an underwater volcano which has emerged four times since 1885 before being dismantled by the ocean. The eastern alignment includes many islands of varying size forming three archipelagoes, Tongatapu (257 km²), Ha'apai (119 km²) and Vava'u (143 km²). The two largest islands of the former are 'Eua and Tongatapu which is the country's largest island on which is situated the capital Nuku'alofa. The Ha'apai archipelago is made up of several minor islands, of which Ha'ano, Foa and Nomuka are the main ones. The Vava'u archipelago is made up of the island of the same name and numerous small islands. Three other islands, situated several hundred kilometers to the north are attached to this group, namely Niuafo'ou, Niuatoputapu and Tafahi which are subject to frequent eruptions on account of very intense local volcanic activity. The two alignments have a very different geological morphology. The western islands have the

# TONGA & NIUE

mountainous and uneven aspect of young, active, andesic volcanoes. Kao peaks at 3,382 feet. The eastern islands, on the other hand, appear as low coral shelves with abundant limestone strata deposited during the Eocene to the Quaternary periods.

## A KINGDOM WHICH HAS ALWAYS MAINTAINED ITS INDEPENDENCE

Descendants of the first Polynesians (doubtless Samoans who came during the 9th-10th Centuries), the Tongan islanders have managed to preserve their independence against wind and tide throughout the ages. The warlike tribes that inhabited the Tongan archipelagoes resisted the numerous Samoan expeditions up to the 12th Century without ever being able to subdue them. The Tongans then enjoyed a period of relative peace, despite local conflicts, until the arrival of the Europeans. They were discovered by the Dutchmen Lemaire and Schouten in 1616 and visited by Tasman in 1643. In the 18th Century, the English rediscovered them through Cook who, won over by the welcome of the inhabitants called them the Friendly islands in 1773. Thanks to the skill of their monarchs who quickly accepted coming to terms with the new arrivals, so as possibly to exact their revenge in the shadows, the Tongans were able to keep their freedom. On the other hand, more than elsewhere in the Pacific, they were subjected to intense evangilization. All types of Christian confessions, starting with Wesleyans and Methodists, swarmed onto the archipelagoes, levelling native cultures. Even today, nothing is done without the agreement of the missionaries or their representatives. The respect of Sunday as a day of rest is absolute. At the beginning of the 19th Century, the kingdom was engulfed in a bloody civil war in which the Ha'apai chiefs attempted to overthrow the reigning Tongatapu family. The English re-established peace but took advantage of the situation to turn Tonga into a British protectorate whilst at the same time retaining the monarchy. In 1958, they granted independence to the country and returned power to the present reigning dynasty, to which the king

◀

*The monumental portico of Ha'amonga,
in the island of Tongatapu, is made up of three
heavy monoliths weigning several tons. It was erected
about 1,200 AD, doubtless for religious purposes, and
took over 1,600 workmen to accomplish the task.*

*Third capital of the kingdom of Tonga,
the site of Mu'a houses the remains
of several royal tombs and ancient fortifications.*

*The flying fox
is a bat which can measure over three feet.
It is the only superior mammal
to have reached the archipelago
without the aid of man.*

Taufa'ahau Tupou IV, son of the popular queen Salote, belongs.

The Christian imprint is particularly marked in Tonga and the religion and morality of the various confessions has submerged the old Polynesian base. The inhabitants have, however, been able to maintain a few of their traditions, such as the hierarchical social structure and some clothing customs. The authority of the clans and their chiefs is everywhere law. Almost all ancient customary systems, the pre-European cults and great myths have, however, disappeared, whereas they are still very much alive in the majority of Polynesian archipelagoes.

## NIUE, THE WILD ISLAND

The archipelago of Niue (or Wild) has a marine surface area of 390,000 km² and is situated between Tonga and Cook islands. It is called the "lost rock" on account of the fact that the main island's coasts, surrounded by several small coral islands, rise sheer and jagged above the ocean. Its impressive and massive structure of 259 km² has a limestone base dating from the Eocene period. At a mean height of 236 feet, the interior plateau is surrounded by a wide shelf measuring some 100 feet. Up to the end of the first millenium, the island remained uninhabited, with just the occasional warfaring expedition from Tonga landing there. Then a small Tongan and Samoan colony settled there episodically. In 1774, when Captain Cook discovered it, there were less than 200 inhabitants who showed themselves to be so aggressive that he gave it the name of Wild island. Forgotten by the rest of the world, their descendants managed to survive by growing taroes, yams and coconuts on the meagre plots of fertile land between the coral rocks. With time, small villages were built along the coast. Today there are twelve of them, including Alofi, the capital. Since 1974, Niue has an autonomous government, even if the island is still closely attached to New Zealand with whom it has signed a free-association agreement. The population of 4,000 fifteen years ago has diminished to under 2,000 as many have left their rocky abode for that of New Zealand.

*Throughout the island,
the multiple varieties
of orchids
light up
the deep forest green
with their colourful
bouquets.*

*The impressive cliffs of*
*Hufangalupe, in Tongatapu,*
*are matched only by those*
*of the eastern coast of Eua.*

*Except in the Buada lagoon, intensive phosphate working in Nauru*
*has only left a small space for coconut groves.*

*The "tapa" is associated with all moments of life.*
*It serves to ornament the inside of houses*
*but also to honour the dead in the surprising*
*and extremely colourful Tongan cemeteries,*
*here that of the Queen's family.*

*The beauty of Tongan women
and above all the purity of their features
had already been noted
by 18ᵗʰ Century European navigators.*

*The daily gathering of mollusks
and mother-of-pearl
on Fahina beach.*

*Lessons are over for these students of the Royal College of Tonga.*
*Each school has its own uniform,*
*a hangover from the period of British administration.*

◄

*The violence of the male "kailao", a war dance,*
*contrasts with the grace of the female "tau'olunga",*
*a very popular solo dance.*

*Quite uncommon in Polynesia,*
*harpoon fishing is, however,*
*currently practised in the Cook islands.*

The vast territory which goes to make up central and eastern Polynesia is the very symbol of what literature for centuries and cinema throughout the 20th Century has presented as the "paradise of the southern seas". The myth of enchanting islands peopled by nonchalant inhabitants with easy-going customs has made us all dream at one time or another and continues to exercise its fascinating charm.

Too often have the Polynesians in this area had to suffer from the image that Europeans have wrongfully created of them. But how is it possible to resist the natural beauty of the Cook islands and French Polynesia, or even the mysteries of Easter island?

## THE COOK ISLANDS, THE ETERNAL TOURIST DESTINATION

The archipelago of the Cook (or Hervey) islands whose total surface area covers 237 km² for a marine surface area of 1,830,000 km², is made up of six small volcanic islands and nine atolls, divided into two groups. The northernmost group includes the atolls of Tongareva (or Penrhyn), Rakahanga, Manihiki, Pukapuka, Nassau, Suwarrow and Palmerston.

The southern group includes the six islands of Aitutaki, Atiu, Mitiaro, Mauke, Mangaia, Rarotonga with the capital of Avarua and the two atolls of Manuae and Takutea.

The atoll base is of Eocene limestone. The islands have a conical volcanic shape, dating from the Tertiary period and are surrounded by a coral reef. The largest is that of Rarotonga, where Mount Te Munga peaks at 2,138 feet.

Up to the last third of the 18th Century, the archipelago remained unknown to Europe, even though the Spanish expedition of Queiros discovered Rakahanga in 1606.

When landing on this island in 1773, Captain Cook called it Hervey before sighting several other islands over his various voyages. The archipelago received his prestigious name. Contacts between British and Polynesians were relatively smooth until 1823 when the Anglican missions arrived. Under their impulse began the systematic destruction of traditional religion and society.

Such abuses gave rise to revolts which were severely crushed. The work was finished by disease and deportations. The original population of the archipelago was reduced by about half. Despite a spectacular demographic recovery since the end of the 19th Century, there are only 20,000 islanders today, of which 80% are pure Polynesians, the rest being made up by various communities (Oceanians, Europeans and Asians). After becoming a British protectorate in 1888, the Cook islands were attached to New Zealand in 1901 before becoming an autonomous state linked to the latter via a free association agreement drawn up in 1965.

Ever since the 19th Century, the Cook islands, particularly Rarotonga and Aitutaki, have attracted visitors in search of an earthly Garden of Eden. Mass tourism brings in thousands of visitors each year, mainly from the U.S. and Japan. The financial manna which the islanders hoped for only rarely filters down to them, however, since it is confiscated by large international groups. To such an extent that, without reaping any noteworthy rewards from their relations with outsiders, the Cook Polynesians on the contrary see their islands invaded by tourists who are gradually destroying their environment and culture. Contaminated by western way of life, they are themselves beginning to lose their soul.

## FRENCH POLYNESIA, PARADISE OF THE SOUTHERN SEAS

Formerly called the French Establishment of Oceania, the French overseas territory of Polynesia encompasses hundreds of islands of varying sizes (for the most part uninhabited) in the south-east Pacific. These are grouped together in five large archipelagoes: Society, Tuamotu, Marquesas, Gambier and the Austral (or Tubuai) islands. Situated 4,300 kms to the north-east of the Marquesas, the uninhabited atoll of Clipperton is attached to the latter but has a long history of dispute between France and Mexico.

French Polynesia covers the most extensive marine surface area in Oceania with 5,030,000 km², of which landmass represents only 4,200 km².

## FIVE ARCHIPELAGOES WITH DISTINCT PERSONALITIES

Each archipelago has its own geological history and therefore a different structure. Three of them, Society, Marquesas and the Austral islands, are of volcanic origin. The other two, Tuamotu and Gambier, are of coral origin.

The Marquesas (1,274 km²) are the summit of an underwater mountain range. They consist of eleven mountain islands (of which only seven are inhabited), numerous islands and the coral island of Clark to the north. The islands are divided into two groups, that to the north-west, which in particular includes Nuku Hiva, the largest island, and Ua Huka, and that to the south-east, which in particular includes the islands of Hiva oa, Tahuata and Fatu Hiva. All of them have a high relief, with certain summits over 3,300 feet and have a jagged appearance on account of active erosion. Recent eruptions, dating for the most part from the Quaternary, have left considerable basalt flows whereas there is practically no evidence of sedimentary formations. Particularly prevalent on the coastline, erosion has been so swift as to give rise to numerous "suspended" valleys, from where rivers spill over into the ocean after a fall of almost 1,000 feet. Another feature of these young islands is the absence of coral barriers and reefs.

The Society islands (1,647 km²) are aligned along a south-east to north-west axis. The archipelago contains fifteen volcanic islands divided into two groups, the Windward islands to the south-east, Makatea, Moorea and Tahiti which is the largest in French Polynesia and houses the capital Papeete, and the Leeward islands to the north-west, Maupiti, Bora Bora, Raïatea, Tahaa and Huahine, which owe their name to the fact that the easterly trade winds reach Tahiti before them. The eruptive formations (in particular basalt flows) which make them up began at the end of the Pliocene age and lasted until the Pleistocene. Between these two eras, a period of violent fracturing with various syenitic intrusions clearly took place. The Society islands have a strongly eroded volcanic aspect. They are high islands with a jagged relief and numerous rocky needles, including Mount Orohena which peaks at 7,350 feet in Tahiti and Mount Tohiea at 3,959 feet on Moorea. They are practically all surrounded by coral reefs whose size is proportional to their age.

The Tuamotu, or Pomotu, archipelago, (915 km²), situated to the east of the Society islands, is the largest in the Pacific. It is made up of sixty or so atolls including Rangiroa, Fakarava, Makemo and Hao which are the largest and a host of small islands stretching over 2,000 kms above a cluster of dorsals which are close together and aligned along a north-west to south-east axis, similar to

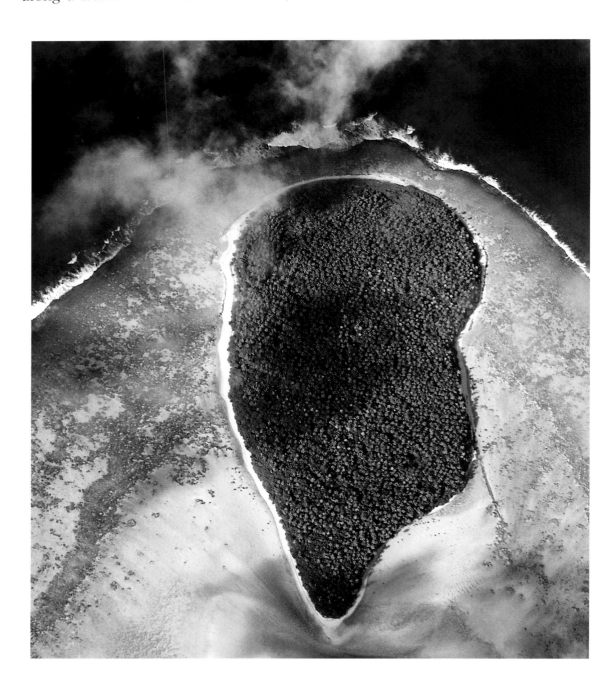

that of the crustal plate movement. The low volcanic base of these atolls (whence the name of Low islands given by Bougainville) and the fact that they stretch out over a considerable distance, means that it has never emerged. They are surrounded by reef formations which are slightly higher than they are. The archipelago is known for being the site of French nuclear testing, strongly contested by international opinion, in the atoll of Mururoa.

The Gambier group is part of the same under-

*One of the small "motu" (coral islands) which make up the paradise atoll of Tetiaroa in the Windward island group.*

water alignment as Tuamotu. In addition to several uninhabited islands, it includes larger ones such as Mangareva. With the exception of the latter, dominated by a compact volcanic mass over 1,300 feet in height, the whole of the

*General view of Bora Bora.*
*The central volcanic mass can be seen together*
*with the barrier reef surrounding the lagoon*
*which has the reputation of being*
*the most beautiful in the Pacific.*

Gambier is of coral formation with a similar structure to those of Tuamotu, to which the archipelago is also attached administratively. The southern Austral archipelago (164 km²) is situated astride the Tropic of Capricorn. There are four major islands, Rurutu, Rimatara, Tubai which gave it its name, Raivavae (or Vavitu), various uninhabited atolls and the island of Rapa 500 kms further to the south. The Austral islands belong to the same underwater volcanic fold as the Cook islands, with which they have a striking structural similarity. With the exception of Rapa with its impressive volcanic relief, high and eroded, and practically without any coral reefs, the Austral islands are low formations surrounded by a wide coral barrier. To the south of Rapa, the hot-spot which is the origin of the whole archipelago is still active. Its last formation was the MacDonald, an underwater volcano today 160 feet below the surface and which should emerge in some 4 million years time.

*Many old traditions,*
*for example the call of the sea-shell*
*or the sculpture on stone of stellar motifs,*
*are brought up to date by new generations.*

*Polynesian dancing, here on the island of*
*Rarotonga, sensually intermingles brusque male*
*with undulating female gestures.*

230

*For two hundred years,*
*the island of Tahiti has made the western world dream*
*and has had almost 13,000 books and articles written about it!*

*The superb bay of Opunohu, in the island of Moorea,*
*is a safe mooring spot,*
*protected by the mountains from ocean fury and storm.*

▶

*Each high island has several microclimates*
*which are conditioned by the lie and height of the relief,*
*bringing rain to one slope whilst the sun shines on another,*
*a situation which can be very rapidly reversed.*

*The rugged aspect of the volcanic formations*
*is witness to the enormous thrust of orogenic forces*
*that occur when islands are born,*
*here near to Teavaro.*

*The tiare*
*is the national flower of the Tahitians.*
*Left to macerate in coconut oil,*
*it gives the sweet-smelling monoã*
*which the islanders rub over*
*their bodies and in their hair.*

*The mountains each have their history.*
*Such as the summit of Moua Puta, in the interior of Moorea,*
*which is pierced by a hole made,*
*according to legend, by the lance of an angry god.*

*The horse was introduced*
*at a late date by Europeans.*
*It is still rare, except in the archipelago*
*of the Marquesas where it has proliferated.*
*Many have returned to a semi-wild state.*

239

*Nature satisfies man's every need for food and shelter.*
*The result is a general feeling of well-being which bestows upon the islanders a cheerful unconcern,*
*as is evident with these "yukelele" players from Huahine.*

## HARSH CONTACTS WITH EUROPEANS

As elsewhere in Oceania, the inhabitants of present-day Polynesia underwent a chaotic history as soon as they came into contact with Europeans. The Tuamotu and Marquesas were the first to be discovered, doubtless by Magellan in 1520, then by the Spaniards Queiros and Torres in 1605, the latter in 1595 by Mendaña who gave the name Marquesas de Mendoza in honour of the viceroy of Peru. After Wallis landed in Tahiti in 1767, followed by Bougainville one year later, the Marquesas received several expeditions, including Cook's in 1774, the American Ingram and the Frenchman Marchand in 1791 who called them the Revolution islands. Gradually the whole of the archipelagoes was discovered, changing name as often as they were discovered. Tuamotu was thus called the Disappointment islands by Byron because he was unable to land there, and the Dangerous archipelago by Bougainville. Attracted by the natural beauty of Tahiti, then called King George island by Wallis, and by the welcome of its inhabitants, Bougainville called the island new Cythera, thereby creating the image of paradise which it has since then retained and which constitutes and ever-real tourist lure.

And yet everything was far from being idyllic in these dream islands following their discovery by the Europeans. According to Cook's estimations, the total population of the different archipelagoes was somewhere around 230,000. At the end of the 19th Century, it was a mere 12,000, no more or less than a frightful hecatomb. The devastating action of unscrupulous Europeans, traffickers, mercenaries, settlers and above all priests who shamelessly initiated a war of religion between English protestants and French catholics, and the introduction of diseases, unknown until then, decimated the natives. The destiny of the islands was sealed in 1847 when Great Britain and France signed a treaty recognizing French protectorate over the territory. In 1880, the last Tahitian king, Pomare IV, abandoned his throne to Paris who immediately took possession of the whole archipelago, which was definitively annexed in 1907. The French administration then took several measures to protect the native populations, but for a long time obliged them to give up their ancient customs.

▶

*The Heiva celebrations in July are the scene of impressive dugout canoe races. The most prestigious have teams of rowers opposing each other over distances of 50 kms.*

*After implanting a graft, the "black-lipped" oyster, the "Pinctada margaritifera", produces the precious black pearl of Tahiti.*

*Contrary to widespread belief, inhabitants of the "Polynesian paradise"*
*observe a relatively strict moral way of life and set great store*
*by the family and faithfulness between husband and wife.*
*Traditional tatooing has come back into favour amongst younger generations.*

*Doubtless brought in from Hawaii a long time ago,*
*the fire rituals fascinate foreigners.*
*They are a hangover from ancient cults that honoured telluric gods,*
*in particular the Queen of volcanoes.*

*The "hi'maa"
is the traditional
Tahitian oven.
Food is wrapped
in palm leaves,
covered in earth
and steamed
for several hours.*

*Each day women
make garlands
and crowns of flowers
for their families.*

## ISLANDERS IN SEARCH OF THEIR ROOTS

The total population of French Polynesia is today 187,550 inhabitants. 67% are Polynesian, 19% Euronesian, 10% Europeans, French for the most part, and the remainder is made up of various Asiatic minorities. This percentage can vary considerably depending on the archipelago. Thus in the Marquesas, Tuamotu, Gambier and the Austral islands whose respective populations total 7,000, 12,400, 650 and 7,500, the Polynesian majority represents at least 80% of the population. In the Society group, on the other hand, where 160,000 people live and where all the non-Polynesian communities are concentrated, the percentage falls to 56%. Everywhere, however, the Polynesians have the same concern: a vehement search after a prestigious past.

Today traditions are regaining ground, particularly amongst the younger generations. The Territory's autonomy in 1956 gave a fillip to the movement of a return to roots. Long, tied-up hair, traditional tatooing, a fresh lease of life for the ancient cults, *marae* (sacred platforms acting as temples) and *tiki*, (effigies of the Oceanian divinity of the same name) have come back in force. The old socio-cultural organizations at village level have been re-instated. For the moment, the Polynesians seem to be negociating the delicate balance between a certain form of return to past values and the demands of modern life. Amongst the multitude of things offered to them in the latter, they choose what is useful to them without renouncing any of their ancestral values which, in their eyes, have been confiscated for too long by France. Numerous claims to independence are being heard and upheld by the majority of Oceanian nations, led by New Zealand and Australia, who do not appreciate one little bit the presence of a European nuclear power in the Pacific.

◀

*Made out of bamboo, pandanus and coconut leaves,
the Tahitian "fare" is gradually disappearing
and being replaced by western-style housing.*

# EASTER ISLAND, ISLAND OF MYSTERY, AND THE CHILEAN ARCHIPELAGOES

Easter island (120 km² of emerged land for 370,000 km² of marine surface), called Rapa Nui, Te Pito o te Henua ("Centre of the world") by the natives, has belonged to Chile since 1888. It is a triangular-shaped island, surrounded by three tiny islands and situated directly over a fracture of the highest part of the South-East Pacific dorsal in the open sea off the Chilean coasts. Essentially volcanic by nature, it is made up of a raised lava triangle (mainly basalt), the angles of which house three extinct volcanoes. The cone of Terevaka is over 1,960 feet in height. The jagged, andesitic coast has no coral barrier. The island is covered, as doubtlessly it was even before the arrival of the first Easter islanders in the 4-5th centuries, by arid moorland, without any water and which has never been able to provide sufficient sustenance for the population, whence frequent famines which were rife on the island when the Europeans landed on Easter Sunday in 1722. Discovered by Roggeveen, it was annexed in 1770 by the Spanish under Felipe Gonzalez. The Europeans found the island inhabited by warlike tribes amidst stone monoliths and petroglyphs created by a civilization of whom they themselves knew practically nothing.

No European power contested the Spanish ownership over the island. On the other hand, Madrid allowed England and France to moor in the main port. The first contacts between natives and Europeans were relatively good. After putting an end to the interminable war which opposed the two major tribal confederations on the island, the "Long Ears" and the "Short Ears", the Europeans introduced livestock and new crops which greatly improved everyone's daily life. The situation degenerated, however, in the 19th Century. Imported diseases caused ravages amongst the population. Missionaries were in open revolt with customary priests. In 1805, the Americans abducted twenty or so men and women from Easter island for seal fishing. From 1860 onwards, Peruvians began to ravage the villages for domestic slaves to work in the mines or on the plantations ending in a revolt by the Easter islanders. Their uprising was, however, disorganized and gave way to ancient tribal rivalries. Repression was bloody. By the end of the 19th Century, when Chile annexed the island, its population had dropped to a mere 100 as against an estimated 4,000 when the Europeans arrived.

*Certain raised statues are over 65 feet in height.*
*The largest weighs 82 tons, not including its 30-ton "pukao".*

Today, an immigration policy set up by Santiago has helped to raise the level once more to about 2,300. The arrival of new blood has, however, deeply modified the Polynesian basis which is difficult to determine on account of the various mixes. Less than 10% of present-day inhabitants are authentic Polynesian Easter islanders, the majority being made up of European, South American and Oceanian mixes. They live in a dozen or so villages along the island's narrow coastal strip. Situated on the western coast, Hanga Roa, the most important, serves as capital. As soon as it was discovered, Easter island hit the

*Modern sculptors have succeeded in preserving the style that is so peculiar to Easter island.*

▶

*Omnipresent in all Easter island mythology, the theme of the bird-man has become a favourite motif with tatooers.*

headlines on account of the dense mystery surrounding its ancient civilization. Multiple statues, strange petroglyphs, tablets engraved with a mysterious writing have enflamed the imagination of scholars and dreamers right down to the present. All kinds of hypotheses have been put forward, including the most fanciful. Some suggested that the first Easter islanders were Amerindians, others saw in the remains proof of extra-terrestrial presence! The most famous works are the *moai kavakava*, giant human busts with a remarkable purity of line, raised on *ahu* (stone platforms), in particular in the zone of Rano Raraku and on the slopes of the sacred volcano Rano Kao. The numerous quarries from which these statues were hewn have been found and it is known that the moai were transported down the mountainous slopes to be placed at sacred places from where they could survey the

ocean. Archeologists and historians have still not agreed on the mode of transport used to move such monuments weighing over several tons on an island which was totally devoid of trees.

The *rongo rongo* (tablets covered with signs assimilated to writing) have still not yielded their secrets, despite modern research techniques. When specialists, noteably Russians and Germans, have deciphered them, doubtless Easter island's mysterious past will teach us a lot about the whole of the Polynesian world.

Chile administers other small archipelagoes in the south-eastern Pacific, situated on the ramifications of the major Pacific dorsal and which reach all the way to the American continent. Their geological nature is identical to that of Easter island. The islands in question are those of Sala y Gomez (0.12 km²) situated 400 kms to the north-east of Easter island, the Desventuradas (the uninhabited islands of San Ambrosio and San Felix have a total surface area of 3.3 km²) and Juan Fernandez (185 km²) which is much nearer to the Chilean coast. Made up of two low shelves whose maximum height does not exceed 100 feet and which are linked by a narrow rocky strip, Sala y Gomez island is difficult to reach. Sometimes it acts as a port of call or a temporary stop-over for fishermen. In the Juan Fernandez archipelago, only one island is permanently inhabited, Mas a Tierra. During the 17th and the 18th centuries it was often visited by filibusters. Today it is called Robinson Crusoe island for it is here that a Scottish sailor named Selkirk was abandoned by his underlings, to be picked up four years later, inspiring the writer Daniel Defoe for his famous novel. Some 250 fishermen, Chilean for the most part, today live around the bay of Cumberland.

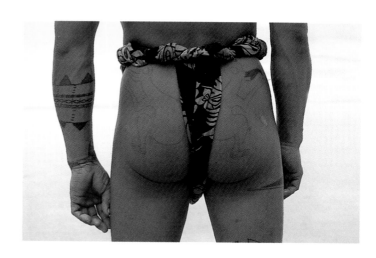

*Although Easter island is in the intertropical zone,*
*its low and offset position make it necessary*
*to wear warm clothing in the early mornings*
*and evenings of the southern winter.*

*Today the statues are aligned*
*on long platforms or "abu".*
*When the Europeans landed on the island,*
*most of them had been knocked over,*
*witness to the violence of the ancient civil war.*

*The region of Putaruru, in the northern island.*

Called Aoteaora by the first inhabitants, the Maori, New Zealand is situated either side of the 40th parallel in the Southern Hemisphere.

For the traveller, it is the opposite of Australia. Whereas the latter is flat, arid and reddish in colour, New Zealand is a country of valleys, woodland and greenery. It has a variety of ever-changing landscapes, from the subtropical bays of the north to the wild Fjordland of the south overlooked by snow-capped peaks, not to mention the volcanoes of the centre.

New Zealand is made up of two main islands, North island (or Smoking island) with the capital Wellington, and South island (or Jade island), aligned along a north-east to south-west axis and separated by the 26 km Cook Strait, together with several small nearby islands (Three Kings, the Snares and Stewart). Situated at hundreds of kilometres from the main islands, other archipelagoes are attached to it, such as the Aucklands, the Antipodes, the Bounty islands, Chatham, Kermadec and Campbell.

The total surface area of New Zealand and its island dependencies is 268,680 km². The country is an independent and sovereign state within the British Commonwealth.

## AN EVENTFUL GEOLOGICAL HISTORY

New Zealand constitutes the southern extremity of the inner Melanesian belt. It is situated on a vast continental shelf stretching for over one million km² beneath the ocean. The emerged landmass of this shelf make up the New Zealand islands. The fact that the morphology of the two islands is very marked may be explained by the slow process of lateral slipping of the inner Melanesian belt formations over a long period from the mid-Jurassic to the Quaternary. Geological structures were disrupted at regular intervals by significant orogenic phases which deeply fractured and uplifted them. The main geological formations are deposits (clays, sandstone) and metamorphic rocks (crystalline schists, gneiss, quartzites, marbles) from the Secondary and Tertiary periods, and volcanic rocks from the Tertiary and Quaternary (granites,

# NEW ZEALAND

porphyrites, basalts). At the beginning of the Cretacious era, the whole of present-day New Zealand underwent strong uplift, particularly in the south island. After this intense orogenic phase, there followed a long period of calm from the Eocene to the Oligocene, during which reliefs were eroded and deposits accumulated in the interior depressions.

A fresh orogenic thrust movement occurred during the Miocene to reach its maximum in the Pliocene during the Kaikoura period. In North island, magma spilled forth in abundance, giving birth to the volcanic formations of the centre and the north, whilst in South island, the impressive range of the southern Alps rose up. During the remainder of the Quaternary era, these reliefs underwent intense erosion. The considerable resulting deposits were the origins of the interior basins and coastal plains.

## GIANT VOLCANIC ISLANDS

The North (114,650 km²) and South islands (154,420 km²) are a succession of impressive parallel mountainous masses which, the nearer one gets to the ocean, rapidly descend towards coastal plains. North island has a 3-fold aspect when approached from north-west to south-east: firstly the Auckland peninsula with its jagged coastline, its low hills reaching a maximum of 2,600 feet, intersected by small alluvial basins, then the volcanic formations of the centre (Mount Ruapehu peaks at 9,175 feet), with its subdued relief and site of intensive post-volcanic activity (smokeholes, sulphur springs, geysers), which stretch around the basin of Lake Taupo, and finally a series of mountain ranges, covered in rich forests, along a north-east to south-west axis (Rakhumara, Huiarau, Ruahine and Tararua), prefiguring the Alps of the South island. Fed by the abundant rainfall and numerous lakes, there is relatively large orographic network with several major rivers (Waikato, Rangitikei, Rangitaiki and Wanganui). South island has a mountainous, high and jagged relief. Despite its height, it is, however, not wide enough to have a large river system. The only two large rivers are the Wairau in the north and the Clutha in the south. On the other hand, there is an abundance of lakes. The southern Alps range is the backbone of the country, with fifty or so summits over 9,800 feet including Mount Cook which peaks at 12,316 feet and some of the largest glaciers in the world, such as the Tasman glacier measuring almost 30 km in length by 2 kms wide. A complex group of secondary ranges surrounds the New Zealand Alps to the north (Spencer, Richmond), east and west. To the south-west, after the depression of Lake Te Anau, the mountains are lower and fragmented into a series of small ranges that slope towards the sea, creating the magnificent fjords of Fjordland.

The islands situated at the southern and eastern extremity of the New Zealand shelf all have a volcanic aspect, comparable to that of the two major islands, but eroded in parts, depending on individual geological history. Summits vary from 3,214 feet for Stewart island (1,735 km²) to 1,050 feet for Chatham island (963 km²).

*Lying at the foot of the Darran Mounts, the superb bay of Milford Sound is considered as the jewel of Fjordland, in the South Island.*

*The temperate ocean climate,*
*with a net tropical influence in the northern part of North Island,*
*gives a rich vegetation with numerous arborescent ferns.*
*Abundant meadow-land supports a 72-million sheep population,*
*here near to Whangarei.*

*Advancing like a spur into the Bay of Plenty,*
*Mount Manganui is important in Maori mythology since it is here*
*that they situate the arrival of numerous ancestral clans.*

*New Zealand has a varied fauna.*
*Animals from tropical and temperate zones exist*
*side by side like these brown blue-beaked gannet*
*and green tree gecko.*

*The region of Mount Tarawera*
*undergoes intense volcanic activity,*
*as witnessed by a multitude of sulphur*
*and smoke holes.*

## A RELATIVELY MILD CLIMATE

The major part of the country has a temperate, oceanic climate giving a relatively large amount of rainfall throughout the year. Laden with Pacific humidity, the westerly winds blow permanently, unlike the episodic warm and dry easterlies from Australia. It is in the more broken relief of North island that the strongest seasonal constrasts may be observed, with abundant winter rain, even if, with regards to rainfall, this is even more marked in the South island which is colder on account of the Antarctic influence. Its southern part has a high mountain climate. The lower limit of the permanent snow, which practically never falls below 8,200 feet on North island, here falls at 6,900 feet. The New Zealand Alps have a high-mountain climate with abundant precipitation (4000 to 5000 mm annually), which explains the exceptional extension of the glaciers that, on the western slopes, come down as far as 1,000 feet above sea level.

## LIMITED FLORA AND FAUNA

The geographical isolation of New Zealand explains why there are relatively few vegetable and animal species on the two islands. Most vegetable varieties are indigenous, even though they have certain similitudes with those of Australia or South America.

There are numerous varieties of palm trees, conifers (*Podocarpus, Dacrydium, Phyllocladus*) and arborescent ferns. The two extremes in vegetation are represented, in the North island, by a Mediterranean brush and a clear, wet forest dominated by giant *kauri* (which can reach 185 feet in height and 50 feet in circumference), *pohutukawa* (or Christmas trees), and in the South island, by the austral forest with abundant beeches and *rimu* (or red pines over 165 feet in height) and which can be found throughout New Zealand. Land situated over 5,000 feet has alpine-type flora.

Fauna is even more limited than flora. If we do not take into account animals brought in by Polynesian man (pigs, dogs, rats) and Europeans (deer, horses, rabbits, stoats and in particular cattle and sheep of which there are today 72 million head), mammals are reduced to only two varieties of bats and south sea creatures include seals, Hooker sea-lions and penguins). Reptiles and amphibians are equally scarce. Certain of them are true living fossils, such as the *tuatara* (or *Sphenodon punctatus*) which is the only reptile from the Secondary period to have survived to the present day. There is, on the other hand, an abundance of bird life and insects, to such an extent that ornithologists have referred to New Zealand as the island of birds.

Many are runner-birds which no longer fly, like the *kiwi* (*Apteryx australis*), the *takahe* (*Notornis mantelli*), the *weka* (*Gallirallus australis*). The most extraordinary specimen was the *moa*, the biggest of which (*Dinornis*) was over 10 feet in height and which definitively disappeared after the arrival of the Maori who mercilessly hunted them.

When New Zealand separated from Gondwana, the main competitors for birds, large grass-eating and carniverous mammals, had not yet reached their population explosion, and left ecological niches vacant which the birds occupied, once they had come down from the trees. Since there was no reason for them to flee, their wings atrophied, which was later to be the reason for their subsequent mass destruction when man arrived on the islands and brought in mammals such as dogs and stoats that killed them.

Amongst indigenous species, the most original are the *kaka*, the *kea* and the *kereru* (or New Zealand pigeon), as well as a variety of giant cricket called *weta*.

*The kiwi has become New Zealand's national emblem. It is a runner-bird which only comes out at night.*

►

*Wakarewarewa park in Rotorua is well-known for its geysers, the biggest of which spurts over 60 feet in height several times per hour.*

*Undergrowth typical of North island forests*
*overgrown by epiphytic plants and giant ferns.*

*Volcanic activity is everywhere present. Numerous small, pungent-smelling lakes*
*offer a palette of different colours depending on the minerals they contain.*

*Maori carving is the most prized in Polynesia.*
*It is carried out both in the prestigious "marae" (community houses)*
*and on domestic objects transformed into works of art, such as these dovecotes.*

# THE MAORI

New Zealand has a population of 3,500,000, 90% of which is of European stock. A small contingent of Asian immigrants (Chinese, Indian) and Arabs (Lebanese, Syrians) represent approximately 1.5%. The remainder is made up by some 300,000 Maori, direct descendants of the Polynesians who peopled the island in the 10th Century AD.

According to tradition, the first Maori arrived successively in long boats from Hawaiki, the original country which certain assimilate with the Marquesas or Samoa.

Again according to tradition, the first Maori navigator to have landed on the eastern coast of North island, leaving from Rarotonga at the beginning of the 10th Century, was called Kupe. Two centuries later, other expeditions led by Toi, Whatonga and Manaia landed on North island. Finally, towards the middle of the 14th Century, there was the "great migration", called the Fleet, from Tahiti, the latter Polynesians imposing their "divine" status over the initial occupants.

## THE BITTER STRUGGLE
## AGAINST COLONIZATION

The Maori's warfaring reputation and legendary aggressiveness are well-known throughout the Polynesian world.

For a long time, Europeans remained far from their coasts, even though Tasman reported them in 1642.

When, after Cook, they landed in the 18th Century, the number of Maori, concentrated particularly in the North island, did not exceed 250,000. The first contacts were quite cold, but did not give rise to any major conflicts. The same could not be said when the British colonization began the following century.

Whalers, missionaries, adventurers of all sorts settled in New Zealand. England sent convicts there as it did to Australia. Immigration reached its height towards 1840.

The treaties signed with the Maori were systematically violated despite the efforts of the British Crown and a series of bloody wars broke out. Already decimated by epidemics brought in by the Europeans, the Maori were massacred in their thousands despite their valour.

They were on the point of disappearing when London imposed strict measures to protect them. In spite of this, their numbers at the end of the 19th Century had dwindled to 42,000.

Since then, a strong demographic progression

has enabled their descendants to reach 300,000 individuals, relatively well integrated into the national community. Many of them live in towns. But others have chosen to live on ancestral lands, particularly in the centre and east of North island. The Waitangi treaty signed in 1840 has enabled them to remain in possession of almost 4 million acres of land.

The autonomy of New Zealand which became a British dominium in 1907, then an independent state within the Commonwealth has given fresh vitality to the Maori soul.

*The Maori were the fiercest Polynesian warfarers*
*that the Europeans had to confront.*
*Today still, the men paint their faces*
*with ritual "moko", stick their tongues out to frighten*
*their enemies and sing impressive "haka",*
*the old war songs.*
*Around their necks,*
*some wear jade "tiki" from South island,*
*called Jade island by the Maori*
*who used to seek the precious stone*
*there in times gone by.*

## AN ART OF THE HIGHEST EXPRESSION

Perhaps on account of their geographical remoteness from the sources of their people, the Maori have developed the most complete art, music and literature of the Polynesian world, highlighting its original characteristics. As if, in an attempt to keep intact the memory of their far-off roots, they cultivate the features to the point of caricature. The most traditional artistic expressions are carvings and bas-reliefs. Such works take the form of in-the-round carvings, ornamental friezes, prow and poop decorations and almost always represent stylized human figures or curvilinear geometrical motifs.

The bas-reliefs generally depict human faces, characterized by a large mouth with a curved top lip, somewhat like a bird's pointed beak. This face is repeated against a background of curvilinear or spiral motifs, comparable to their carved counterparts. Maori music is above all popular with all the characteristics of eastern Polynesian music. Epic songs recounting the exploits of the gods or heroes are often the accompaniment to dances. Amongst the latter, the most famous are the different *haka*, powerful war songs meant to strike fear into the enemy. Maori literature is based on Polynesian myths but gives them a much greater scope, filling in particularly the gaps left by other traditions. The narratives are grouped in vast cycles which are not without recalling the cyclical accounts of medieval Europe.

One of the most famous heroes is a trickster called Maui, a civilizer who preferred men to the gods. Slowing down the course of the sun so as to lengthen the day, parting the sky and the earth so as better to breathe, bringing man fire and useful plants, he finally perishes by wanting to give them immortality. His innumerable adventures were originally part of the heritage reserved for the aristocratic class of Maori priests. Today they have become a sort of anthology of popular wisdom with which all New Zealand children are familiar.

*In Maori tradition,*
*totems have a great importance*
*as they represent the spirits of gods and ancestors.*
*They are placed at the entry of villages or along roads to protect inhabitants.*

*Hawaii, nicknamed Big Island by the Americans, is the largest island in the archipelago.*

# 6

## 6

# HAWAII

Hawaii is the most northerly of the Polynesian archipelagoes and is the 50th state of the United States. It is made up of eight main islands, Hawaii (the most recent and the largest which gave its name to the archipelago), Maui, Kahoolawe, Lanai, Molokai, Oahu (on which is situated the capital Honolulu), Kauai and Niihau, bordered by several small islands aligned along a south-east to north-west axis over a large sub-oceanic fold whose western extremity is marked by the island of Kaula and which extends the underwater Emperor Sea Mounts to the south. To the south-east of Hawaii, above the hot-spot which still feeds the island, as it does the whole of the archipelago, a new island is rising towards the surface and should emerge in some millions of years time. The Americans have already found a name for it: Loihi. The total surface area of the islands is 16,700 km² for a marine surface area of 2,160,000 km².

## AN ALIGNMENT OF VOLCANOES

Aligned along a north-west to south-east axis, all the Hawaiian islands are of volcanic origin. Extinct or active cones abound. The general structure of the islands is made up of a super-position of numerous basalt flows which took place particularly in the Quaternary period and which gave rise to impressive reliefs. Subjected to highly active erosion and abundant rainfall, the latter have been gradually worn away. They become lower as they go from the south-east to the north-west, in the direction of crustal plate movement. Thus from the highest point which is in the island of Hawaii at 13,792 feet, the height drops to 10,020 feet in Maui, 5,170 in Kauai and 1,280 in Niihau. The western, and therefore the oldest, volcanic formations are often reduced to simple atolls, whilst at the east rises the impressive mass of the island of Hawaii, the last to appear. It is made up of five shield volcanoes, the two largest of which are Mauna Kea (13,792 feet) and Mauna Loa (13,678 feet). Although slightly lower, the latter, with a base situated some 18,000 feet below the sea and a diameter of over 1,300

feet, is the largest volcano on earth. It is also the most active of Hawaiian volcanoes, particularly since the mid-nineteenth century, and erupts regularly. The eruptions of 1942, 1974 and 1985 were particularly devastating. These last few years, another cone, Kilauea, has been even more violent. After shedding torrents of lava in 1990, it is once more in a period of eruption.

## A STRONGLY CHARACTERISTIC CLIMATE

The off-centre position of the Hawaiian archipelago, situated on the Tropic of Cancer, gives it a climate with wider seasonal variations than in the rest of Polynesia, with the exception of New Zealand. Tempered by the north-east trade winds, mean summer temperatures do not exceed 26°C. In winter they vary around 21°C. Rainfall is abundant. Exposed to the ocean winds, the north-east slopes receive between 4,000 and 6,000 mm of water per year, and in some parts (Kauai for instance) up to an annual 15,000 mm! The south-west slopes on the other hand receive little rain, on average between 100 and 300 mm. The seasons have relatively little influence on rainfall, most of which is determined by the height and shape of relief.

Such a greenhouse atmosphere gives rise to a luxuriant, tropical-type vegetation on most of the archipelago. Superb species can be found there, some of which are sought after for their value like sandalwood or the gigantic *koa* (or Hawaiian mahogany). In the lower, drier regions, it gives way to a patchy forest where the *hau* (hibiscus) and thespesias (portia tree) are the dominant plants. Coastal areas are covered by savana grassland which abounds in spiky bushes. There are some interesting native species of fauna, such as the laughing spider, the dragonfly, the *elepaio* (fly-catcher) and the *iiwi* (honey-eater). Some are in the process of disappearing like the *nene* (or Hawaiian goose), the *io* (or Hawaiian sparrowhawk) and the *opeapea*, a bat which is doubtless the only mammal to have peopled the archipelago not to have been introduced by man.

▲

*The island of Oahu has been radically transformed by the American way of life.*
*Only the western coast, inhabited for the majority by people of Polynesian stock*
*has succeeded in retaining a part of its authenticity,*
*here in Makaha.*

*The immense lava flows*
*from the numerous eruptions*
*of Kilauea from 1969 to 1974,*
*then from 1983 to 1990,*
*descend towards the ocean*
*from Apua to Waha'ula*
*Heiau.*

*The volcano*
*is in permanent activity.*
*The molten lava runs*
*through underground tunnels*
*and finishes up*
*in the bubbling sea.*

# AN UNTRACEABLE POLYNESIAN IDENTITY

Polynesians, for the most part of Samoan and Tahitian origin, were living in the Hawaiian archipelago when Cook discovered it in 1778, two centuries after it had been sighted by the Spanish. Won over by the welcome of the inhabitants and the enchanting surroundings, the English captain estimated that "some 300,000 individuals at least... were leading a wild and healthy life... in the Sandwich islands" (name of the First Lord of the Admiralty). Which didn't prevent them from killing him the following year. In 1855, a census counted 65,000 Hawaiians. By the end of the nineteenth century they numbered a mere 45,000, which represented a huge demographic drop. The usual factors accompanying such a phenomenon are, alas, well-known: disease imported from Europe, massacres, deportations, colonization, evangelization... But there is another which is specific to the Hawaiian archipelago and which explains this abnormally high rate of human loss.

On the arrival of the Europeans, the islanders were disunited. Although the archipelago was dominated by a dynasty of powerful kings, the various islands had not been able to set up a single socio-cultural system, or at least one which referred to a set of values common to other Polynesians.

Each group worked out its own political system, which was sometimes complex, always extremely hierarchical, and which it could not or would not share with its neighbours. Inter-island wars were frequent. This Hawaiian "scattering" played into the hands of the conquerors, settlers and missionaries who exacerbated the divisions in order to rule. But it was in 1875 that the fate of Hawaii was decided.

With the reigning family of the main island, the Americans signed a commercial agreement regarding the export of sugar, but which in reality handed over to them the archipelago's economy. Immediately numerous immigrants arrived from Europe, Japan, China and above all from the U.S. The population tripled in twenty years and the Polynesian identity of the Hawaiians began to melt rapidly. Events quickly succeeded each other.

After queen Liliuokalani had been removed from the throne, the monarchy was replaced by a republic under the wing of the Americans in 1894. In 1898, the archipelago was annexed by the United States to become in 1959 the fiftieth State. To begin with, the American way of life finally buried the remaining Polynesian customs. Literally phagocyted by a cosmopolitan human group, urbanized (88% of the population live in a town), Americanized to excess, the Hawaiian people melted in the mass. Almost 1,300,000 people live in Hawaii, making it the most populous archipelago in Oceania. 87% are of non-Polynesian origin, including a large number of Whites (35% of the population), Japanese (25%), other Asians (13% Chinese, Koreans and Philippinos), numerous mixes and various Oceanians.

The 170,000 Polynesians represent only 13% of the population. And yet, since the 1970s, ancient traditions are resurging. Often isolated in remote areas of the islands and removed from the Americano-Japanese majority, stock Hawaiians seem to have rediscovered their ancestral values. Thus pre-European cults and rites are re-appearing, such as the offerings to Pele, goddess of the volcanoes or wedding ceremonies carried out by the customary priest. *Tapu* (taboo) places are again respected. But unlike what is happening in French Polynesia, the younger generations are not wholeheartedly behind their parents.

The survival of the Hawaiian soul, and perhaps finally the creation of a Hawaiian entity, will depend on the choice that the archipelago makes, at the beginning of the third millenium, between the American mirage and Polynesian authenticity.

*Some of the numerous petroglyphs carved by the first Polynesians into the soft lava. Many, alas, have already been covered by the ceaseless flow of magma.*

Ancient cults have been re-appearing
over the past fifteen years.
The Hawaiian soul is regaining strength
thanks to the efforts of younger generations.
Like others, this native priest of Waimea has renewed
with the past and is transmitting tradition.

The powerful Tu,
the Polynesian god of war,
called Ku in Hawaii.

*A few ancestral rituals, such as this greeting to Pele, goddess of volcanoes,*
*are once more being practised after a long period of oblivion.*

▶ *The alignment of the Hawaiian islands is marked by a succession of extinct volcanoes. In Oahu, they form the compact mass of the Koalau Mounts which make up the backbone of the island.*

*Frigates live in peaceful areas of the lesser populated islands, here in Lanai. The males swell their red pouch during courting displays. The fledglings are covered in thick white down.*

*Massive de-forestation of the islands has decimated Hawaiian birdlife. In order to replace it, inhabitants have imported new species that proliferate quickly, such as these spotted doves.*

# CONCLUSION

At the dawn of the 21st Century, the Pacific is called on to become the new pole of the world. On both sides of the great expanse are most of the major powers of today and tomorrow: to the east Canada, the U.S. and Mexico, to the west Russia, China, Japan, Australia and, not far away, Taiwan and Indonesia. The Pacific offers numerous perspectives for the future in the shape of its natural space, its halieutic resources, and the mineral riches of its ocean floor. The third millenium cannot do without the mechanical energy of tides and waves, nor the thermal energy of the waters, nor the multiple underwater biological matter.

Under the impetus of the Americans and Russians in the 50's, the displacement of the geostrategic and political world centre towards Oceania has gathered momentum since 1965, with the forceful entry of Japan, Australia and New Zealand, then to a lesser degree, the Canadians and the Indonesians. Taken unawares, the Europeans have tried to keep contact by developing their possessions, whether admitted or not, in this zone, the French in particular in their overseas territories and the British via the institution of the Commonwealth.

Competition is tough between all these industrial powers who are eager to get the lion's share. Such competition is in three fields: economic, politico-strategic and cultural. For the moment

the two main protagonists in this "war" are the United States and Japan, particularly since the implosion of the Soviet bloc. In the short term, the Pacific risks becoming an American "lake" managed by Japan.

And what of the Oceanians in all this? If we can hold out reasonable hope for a more or less acceptable near future for Micronesians, drawn into the Americano-Japanese orbit, and Polynesians, under American and French influence, since they represent the image of those tropical paradises much sought after by westerners, what will be the fate of the Australian Aborigines, Papuans and other Melanesians who attract neither the investor

nor the tourist, in short all the populations of the western Pacific? Native economies are based essentially on agriculture. But with the exception of useful plants that supply the food for different populations and which consequently bring in nothing from a financial point of view, all those from which an income may be derived (copra, banana, coffee and cocoa trees) are threatened by substitute products that have caused a collapse in the market rates. In addition, the operations in these fields are run by large overseas companies who receive the largest part of the dividends. With regards to the riches under the sea-floor, the situation is even worse.

None of these countries has the technical or financial means to exploit its own resources, whence the call on international cartels who deprive local populations of the profits which they had hoped to see. Thus it is that Vanuatu sees its manganese disappear, the Solomon islands their copper and phosphates, Fiji its gold, New Caledonia its nickel, Bougainville its copper...

Such international plundering in which all the industrialized countries without exception take part can only lead to increased poverty of countries which are said to be independent but which in reality live under the shadow of a "big brother" with a vested interest. In the long run, the subsequent feeling of injustice and the negation of native cultures, often relegated to the level of cute folklore, can only lead to violent confrontations of a colonial type amongst those who are still under foreign ward or who feel dispossessed of their ancestral land, as witness the recent bloody events in Bougainville and New Caledonia.

The Pacific islanders seem to have few trump cards to play when it comes to avoiding the steam-roller process of American, Japanese or European normalization.

The problems of native identity can only issue in a cruel dilemma: submit to the general order and lose the ancestral way, or resist and risk disappearing sooner or later. Many Oceanians are clearly aware of the stakes, but what can you do when you are under the control of a foreign power? Today there are only 11 sovereign states: Australia, Papua New Guinea, the Solomon Islands, Vanuatu, Fiji, Kiribati, Nauru, Tuvalu, Western Samoa, Tonga and New Zealand. And yet all Oceanian people have tried to react at an international level. They have grouped themselves into two regional organisations, the South Pacific Conference and the South Pacific Forum. The former was set up in 1947 and its seat is in Nouméa in New Caledonia. Regardless of their political status, all Pacific States have belonged to it since 1962. It looks into problems of health, nutrition, the environment and regulation of fishing quotas and zones. But it does not contribute to the major international debates as it is muzzled by the great powers. It was in order to remedy this situation that the second organisation was set up in 1971.

The seat of the South Pacific Forum is in Suva, in Fiji. Despite blocking tactics and pressures, it tries to tackle the real problems

of Oceania head-on, such as the multiple political and economic claims of its first inhabitants, the Oceanians.

The record is somewhat pessimistic. How could it be anything else in a world where the computer hounds away genies, where the cult of reason kills mystery, where profit makes the ancestral tradition of doing things for nothing seem ridiculous? And yet history is never written before it happens and can sometimes reserve surprises.

Perhaps the Aborigines, the New Guineans, the Melanesians, the Micronesians and the Polynesians will find the material means to preserve their exceptional cultures. The spiritual means they already have.

*The author wishes to thank all those who helped him during the fifteen years it took to take the photographs
and collect the information that went into the production of this book.
His gratitude goes in particular to the following people and organisations:*

Bill ACKER, Olivier BRIAC, Vetea BAMBRIDGE, Ken FERRIS, Taiana GARCIA,
Ilesa Ratuva GONEWAI, Alex LEINHARDT, Ines de LOUBENS, Wilson C.MAELAUA,
John E.H. MARSH MBE, Teiki PAMBRUN, Regina and Eric RIDET, Véronique and François SARANO, Teva SYLVAIN and his family,
His Royal Highness TAURA'AHAU TUPOU IV, King of TONGA, Merian TUPOU and her family,
Poagou TCHIDOUANE and her family, Leone YARAGAMUDU, all the inhabitants of the village of TIKI,
all the inhabitants of the villages of BAYUN, OTSJANEP, ANGGURUK, OPAGIMA, LAULASI, OMARAKANA, MALAWAI.

The Territorial Assembly of French Polynesia
The Cultural Center at Pacific Harbour (Fiji)
The Cultural Center at Lapita (New Caledonia)
The Land Councils of Queensland and Western Australia
Northern Territory Tourist Commission (Australia)
The Ministries for Cultural Affairs of Tonga, the Solomon Islands, Kiribati, Western Samoa, the Federated States of Micronesia
Walmea Valley Park, Wal O Tapu Park (New Zealand), Whakarewarewa Park (New Zealand)

Graphic realisation
BOWER

Photocomposition, execution and cartography
PLEIN FORMAT
Marseille, France

English version
IAN TRICKETT LANGUES VIVES
Bourdeilles, France